LIFE IN MARSHALL

By

Sandra Gowing

Do you have a story to tell? What's your animal spirit? Share it with us. #hellobeesties

Wildebeest
Publishing Co.

Wildebeest Publishing Company, LLC
6456 Collamer Road
Syracuse, NY 13057

For more information about copyrights and usage, special discounts on bulk purchases, workshops, and engagements, please contact Wildebeest Publishing Company, LLC at (315) 220-0217, info@wildebeestpublishing. com, or online at www.wildebeestpublishing.com

Wildebeest Publishing Company, LLC Paperback First Edition August 2023, United States of America

Cover art by Emma Warren
Illustrations by Isabella Gowing

ISBN 978-1-958233-17-7

For my sister

Judith Baldwin

TABLE OF CONTENTS

PROLOGUE

I sat on the porch swing on a warm summer morning, feeling the sun on my face as I used my feet to gently move the swing back and forth. My little world in the small town of Marshall, Michigan was quiet and peaceful, a good place to be a kid in the summer of 1953. Of course, there were problems in the greater world even then, but the ones we would later face – issues like climate change and the COVID-19 pandemic – were far in the future and could not have been imagined by a ten-year-old girl who had just completed the fifth grade and saw only an endless summer vacation stretching out in front of her.

My thoughts that morning, as I waited for my sister Judy to finish her breakfast and join me on the swing, were centered around my activities for that day. There were so many choices! We could head across our backyard and enter the deep cut where we would spend part of the day running along its paths, among the many trees and bushes. We might walk to the Capitol Hill School playground or the County fairgrounds where we always found something interesting to do. If it were allowance day, we would head down the hill to Freddie's market and choose from their large selection of penny candy.

We might just wander around our neighborhood, looking for whichever friends happened to be around, or walk downtown where we could sit on the chairs at Morris's 5 & 10 and read the latest issues of our favorite comic books. Perhaps we would hop on our bikes and ride all over town, not knowing where we would end up. The possibilities were endless on that summer day in 1953 and life was good.

CHAPTER 1
GRAMPA OSBORN

Grampa Osborn was in his seventies when I first met him and my initial impression was of a cranky old man who didn't seem to like kids very much. He was a slightly built man with a bushy gray mustache and a somewhat stooped posture. He rarely smiled and I don't remember ever hearing him laugh. Most of the time his features were firmly set in a disagreeable expression. His fingers were stained a yellowish brown from the tobacco he chewed and he always seemed to have a wad of it stuck in his cheek.

He walked slowly and painfully due to what he called his "rheumatism." Grampa was hard of hearing and one needed to speak loudly when talking to him. His most prominent feature was a badly shaking right hand due to apparent nerve damage caused by a fall from a silo years earlier. This presented the biggest problem when eating or drinking. A tablecloth usually couldn't be used for more than one meal. This messy process probably could have been avoided if he had only learned to eat with his left hand but it seems he never did. Grampa was a simple man, with little formal education and limited knowledge of the world beyond the boundaries of his own rural life and, it's possible, that it never occurred to him to try.

Claude Osborn was my step-great-grandfather, having married my great-grandmother, Nellie, when she was a widow with two young boys, one of whom was my mother's father. Because they lived in Marshall, Michigan and my family lived in Buffalo, New York, I knew the Osborns mostly through letters and gifts sent at Christmas. We did make one trip to visit them and, when Nellie died, we drove there for the funeral. Soon after her death, we moved to Marshall. Grampa needed someone to look after him and he offered to sign his house over to my parents in return for them making the move. As they had been renters in Buffalo, this would be a step up for them.

Grampa had an elderly sister and brother living in town but, otherwise, had no living relatives other than us and my mother's younger sister, who lived on a dairy farm in upstate New York with her family. My mother's father and Nellie's other son from her first marriage had both died as young adults. The two children who had come out of Claude and Nellie's marriage had died during childhood, their son at only a few months, and their daughter, Agnes, at age 15. I don't remember Grampa talking about them except for those times when something would be mentioned that would remind him of Agnes, after which he'd speak briefly about something she liked or did. Although few words were spoken, it was clear from the tone of his voice and a softening of his facial expression that he loved her very much.

A framed picture of Agnes sat on a small table in Grampa's bedroom. My sister and I both remember her as a pretty girl with Down syndrome features and, although I never heard that term used, I remember my parents saying Agnes "wasn't right." On the wall near his bed hung a single ear of corn and my mother once told me that Agnes had been holding it when she died. The husks had been pulled down to make a skirt and I think she had probably been using it for a doll at a time when there wasn't much money to buy toys. Her obituary said she died at home of a streptococcal sore throat infection.

My sister and I didn't like Grampa very much and he didn't seem to like us either. When he spoke to us it was usually to criticize something we did or tell us that he never did things like that when he was young. I now regret that I didn't talk to him more. He could have told me a lot, not only about his own life but about my mother's family. At the time, I wasn't interested. We talked a little but mostly ignored each other. He was used to a quiet house and we were noisy. He liked my sister more than me. Judy was three years younger than me and cute. I was a skinny, awkward kid at an age when I "knew everything." I remember him once giving Judy a dollar for her birthday when my birthday had recently come and gone with no acknowledgment from him. He didn't seem to be aware that my feelings were hurt, and I pretended not to care.

Grampa was old-fashioned and set in his ways. He was critical of many of the things we did and the way we did them. On the rare occasion my mother might sit for a few minutes and read a magazine, he would say, "In my day, women didn't have time to do that." He still shaved with a straight razor. His shaving cup and brush sat on the bathroom shelf and his razor strap hung from a hook on the door. How he managed to shave with his shaking hand is a mystery. Of course, it never occurred to me to ask him and, had I done so, would have undoubtedly been told by my mother to mind my own business. Grampa hated chicken and refused to eat it. He once told us he had lived on a chicken farm during the Depression and ate it for every meal. Whenever we had chicken, my mother would prepare something else for him.

Grampa spent most of his day in a rocking chair sitting near the window. He didn't have a television and was disapproving when ours was moved in. This was 1952 when television was still quite new and we were all very taken by it. After supper, we would turn it on and spend the entire evening watching it. The minute it went on, Grampa would get up out of his chair, go into his room, and shut the door. His room was right off the living room and my mother would caution us to be quiet so as not to disturb him, but being the ages we were, that wasn't easy and I think we were probably pretty loud. We always thought Grampa secretly watched TV when we were all out as sometimes we would come home to find him just leaving the living room.

4

One of us would put our hand on the top of the television, smile and say "Yep, it feels warm." We knew he had been watching it.

Grampa had an old rattletrap of a car which he refused to give up.

My father wanted him to sell it, saying "I can drive you anywhere you want to go," but Grampa didn't want to part with his car.

Most of the time, the car sat in the garage but once in a while, to my parents' distress, he would take it out for a drive. With his poor vision and hearing, limited mobility, and shaking hand, he was an unsafe driver and a menace to all others on the road. On two occasions during the time Grampa lived with us, he was involved in accidents, one a minor fender bender, but the other more serious, causing damage to two parked cars. While nobody was injured, Grampa was cited by the Marshall police for reckless driving, and his car was badly damaged. This ended his driving days, much to my parents' relief.

Grampa had two cats and a dog when we moved in with him. Pets were a new thing for my sister and me. In Buffalo we lived in a large housing project that had been built for the "war workers" – the people who moved to Buffalo to work in the aircraft and munitions factories during World War II – and animals weren't allowed. Tiger and Goldie, the two cats, were somewhat aloof, but friendly enough and we immediately took to them. They weren't lap cats but allowed us to pet them. Sometimes we played with them, getting them to chase a length of yarn or string. Most of the time, they stayed out of our way, but on a couple of occasions, we managed to snatch them up and attempted to dress them in our doll clothes and push them around in our toy carriage. They refused to put up with this, thrashing about until escaping and running off with the clothes trailing behind them. Grampa summoned them to supper every evening, calling out "kitty, kitty" in a high-pitched voice, after which they would appear from somewhere and devour their meals. What eventually became of Tiger and Goldie, I don't remember. They spent much of their time outside and perhaps one day they simply didn't return home.

Skeeter was a mangy black dog who was kept tied up out back. We were told to stay away from him as he wasn't used to kids and might bite us. Judy and I would sit on the back steps watching him while he warily eyed us from a distance. As time went by, he drew closer and eventually let us pet him. He was then let off the rope and we became good friends. Although he spent most of his time outdoors, my parents began letting him into the house at night and during inclement weather. They weren't thrilled with Skeeter. He smelled bad and often barked and snarled at people. They were always worried that he would bite someone. They more or less tolerated him because he was Grampa's dog.

Skeeter soon became our dog and went everywhere with

us. There were no leash laws in those days (or if there were, they weren't enforced) and many dogs just roamed all over the place. Skeeter was an aggressive dog and sometimes got into fights with other male dogs. We had always been told not to go near fighting dogs, so when this happened, we would stand back, watching them going at each other furiously until the fight ended. Skeeter hadn't been neutered and was probably responsible for increasing the Marshall dog population. He was protective of Judy and me, and if another kid showed any aggression toward either of us, even in play, he would growl and bark at him. Although our friends weren't really afraid of Skeeter, they all had a healthy respect for him, immediately backing off at the first bark.

Skeeter followed Judy and me to most of the places we went and would wait patiently outside any place that he couldn't enter. We sometimes walked places with our mother and when he tried to follow us she would admonish him to stay back. He would sit in the yard watching us go, but after we had been walking for a time, Judy and I would look back to see him skulking along at a distance. When we came out of whatever store or house we had visited, there he would be, waiting for us. He often followed us to school in the morning but would find his way home, seeming to know we would be there for several hours.

Skeeter liked to hang around the kitchen at suppertime and, if my mother didn't shoo him outside, would park himself under the table while we ate. Both Judy and I were poor eaters who often needed prodding to finish our supper, especially foods we didn't really like. Although Mom had told us "Don't feed the dog from the table," when we thought nobody was looking, we'd sneak bits of our food to Skeeter who seemed to like everything.

We had Skeeter for most of the five years we lived in Marshall. As he got older, he became testier and more unpredictable. My parents eventually had him euthanized after he reportedly bit, or threatened to bite, a little girl, the daughter of someone who had stopped by the house to talk to one of them.

We weren't home when the incident occurred and the details were sketchy but we were told by my father that the child had reached out to pet Skeeter and he "went after her for no reason."

He then said, "We can't have a dog who is going to bite kids."

They had immediately taken him to the vet where he was "put to sleep." So that was that. Skeeter was gone, having exited our lives as quietly and unexpectedly as he had entered them.

Grampa Osborn never knew that Skeeter died because he had died himself by that time. We were told one day that Grampa was sick and needed to go live at his sister Nora's house where it would be quieter. A few days after that, we came home from school to discover he had left, taking all his belongings. The shaving things, the ear of corn, the picture of Agnes all were gone and I never saw any of them or him again.

My father told us he had asked Grampa if he wanted to take Skeeter with him to Nora's house, but Grampa had said no, "He's the girls' dog now."

Later that spring, Nora called to tell us Grampa had died. I attended the funeral with my parents, but Judy didn't go. They thought she was too young and didn't think she should miss school. Sitting through the service, only half listening, my ears perked up when I heard the minister speak of a "loving granddaughter" who had placed a flower in the coffin. Knowing that it could only have been Judy, I asked her about it later. She told me that it had indeed been her. Miffed at being excluded from the funeral, and determined to acknowledge Grampa's passing in some way, she and a friend had secretly called at the funeral parlor during the off hours. She picked a tulip from a nearby garden and placed it in the coffin.

I probably wouldn't have thought of doing anything like that. I was a teenager by that time and interested mostly in myself and my own world of friends and school. Grampa's passing didn't seem to affect my life very much. Looking back now, I can see what a hard life he had and the many losses he suffered but, at that time, those thoughts never occurred to me. A few months after he died, my parents sold our house and we moved back to New York. Sixty years would pass before I would return to Marshall.

CHAPTER 2
MOVING TO MARSHALL

I moved to Marshall, Michigan in the summer of 1952 when I was about to turn ten years old. Until then, I had lived in Buffalo, New York, where I was born. My great-grandfather, Claude Osborn, had lost his wife that spring and, being elderly and frail, didn't feel able to manage on his own. When he asked my parents to move in with him in exchange for transferring ownership of his home to them, they agreed and so it followed that, at the end of the school year, our family of four made the 400-mile move to Marshall.

Marshall is in South Central Michigan, not far from the border with Indiana. If one were to hold up a hand in the shape of a mitten, Marshall would be in the center of the fatty pad of tissue, just below the palm and near the thumb. At the time I lived there, it had a population of about 5,000. The closest city of any size was Battle Creek. About 12 miles away, it was the home of the famous cereal companies, Kellogg's and Post.

Marshall was founded in 1830 by brothers Sidney and

George Ketchum. The town had at one time hoped to become the state capitol and went so far as to build a Governor's mansion, but when the issue was put up for a vote in 1847, the state legislature decided to make Lansing the capitol. Marshall was a sleepy little town and not much happened there until 1912, when Harold C. Brooks took over his family business, The Brooks Rupture Appliance Company. The Brooks company was located in Marshall and had become very successful by making supportive devices for those with hernias.

Mr. Brooks not only ran the company but also became greatly involved in the community, eventually becoming its greatest patron. He was elected mayor in 1925 and was responsible for making many improvements. He built the town hall, fire and police stations, paying 90% of the cost himself. He also built the Brooks Memorial Methodist Church and planted and cared for trees all over the city. He encouraged city beautification by awarding prizes for the best lawn, garden, and home restoration. In 1930 he built a large Greek Revival fountain at the edge of town as a centennial gift to the people.

At the time I lived in Marshall, the Brooks family still lived there, occupying a large mansion somewhere across town from where we lived. They were spoken of as "the richest family in town" and there were several stories told about them. One of the most prevalent rumors was that they gave out full-size candy bars on Halloween. Whether it was true or not, I never found out. Although we always vowed to go there on Halloween night, we never made it. We weren't exactly sure where the Brooks mansion was and were always too tired after the night of trick or treating to try to find it.

Harold C Brooks left his stamp on Marshall and many things there were named after him. It was an idyllic, small mid-western town, full of lovely homes and big old trees. The Kalamazoo River ran through it and intersected with Rice Creek. There were pretty parks and, scattered around the town, were stone drinking fountains that bubbled up a constant supply of cold water.

Michigan Avenue was a thriving downtown business district and had a large variety of stores. There were dress shops, hardware stores, restaurants, and drug stores with soda fountains where one could get a cherry or lemon coke for five cents. There was a five and ten-cent store and two movie theaters. The Garden Theater was the one where kids paid ten cents' admission to watch Roy Rogers or the Bowery Boys on a Saturday afternoon. The Bogar was a more grown-up theater that showed regular first-run movies and charged fifty cents for adults and twenty-five cents for those under twelve. On Eagle Street, just south of downtown, stood Schuler's Restaurant, known all over Michigan for its fine food.

Just to the west of downtown was the circle which contained the beautiful Brooks Memorial fountain, which stood several feet high and spewed out jets of water that were lit up at night with colored lights. There were several benches surrounding the fountain and it was a popular place to go in the evening. On pleasant summer nights, several people could usually be found sitting there, gazing at the fountain as if watching a miracle unfold.

My sister Judy and I wandered all over that first summer, exploring the town. We discovered the county fairgrounds, the Capitol Hill school playground, and we found a construction site where a new community building was being built to be a great place to play. Our wanderings took us past a school-yard where a group of kids was learning to twirl batons. When we stopped to watch, we were invited to join the lessons, which were free. We continued them through the whole summer and had a lot of fun. We met a lot of kids our age and got to know Marshall in a way that made it seem as if we had never lived anywhere else. Indeed, by the end of the summer, we had mostly forgotten about Buffalo. Marshall was now our home.

(Information for the above chapter was acquired from the following article: "Marshall, A Town Heavy on Charm" by John J. Collins, Chicago Tribune – September 4, 1988)

CHAPTER 3
710 SOUTH MARSHALL AVENUE

My grandfather's house was at 710 South Marshall Avenue, on a hill located between the Kalamazoo River and Rice Creek. This hill was sometimes called Capitol Hill as it was in the part of town where the governor's mansion had been built at the time when Marshall was hoping to become the Michigan state capitol.

The house we lived in was, at the time, over seventy years old, having been built in 1880. It had leaded glass windows and an open front porch with a two-person swing hanging on metal chains from the roof. The front door had a skeleton key, but the only time we locked it was on the rare occasions that we took a week-long vacation to visit relatives in New York. Most of the time we left the house unlocked.

The inside of the house was in poor condition with an old-fashioned kitchen and bathroom. The house had "settled" so the floors were uneven. It was located a short distance away from some railroad tracks and whenever a fast-moving train ran through, the whole house shook.

The bathroom was downstairs and had an old-fashioned clawfoot tub. A door off the kitchen led to a dirt floor cellar with an old coal furnace and coal bin. My grandfather's bedroom was downstairs, off the living room, with the other bedrooms being located on the second floor. The three upstairs rooms were accessed by a curved staircase off the dining room. My sister and I shared one room and my parents another. The remaining small room became our playroom as it had a heat register which our bedroom didn't have.

Our room was frigid in the winter, especially at night when the coal fire died down. We woke early each winter morning to the sounds of my father shoveling coal into the furnace and went to sleep to the clanging and banging sounds as he "banked" the fire for the night. On school mornings, my mother would call up the stairs, "Time to get up for school." We'd then grab our clothes and run downstairs to dress in the warmer kitchen or bathroom.

The inside of the house was in terrible condition, suffering from years of neglect, the Osborns being infirm and unable to properly care for it. It needed a great deal of work and while my parents did some painting and wallpapering, they couldn't really afford to do extensive remodeling, so we mostly just lived in it as it was. My parents' room had the only closet in the house, so my father fashioned one for our room out of old curtains and curtain rods. Clothes were also kept in a metal wardrobe in the upstairs hall and coats and boots were kept in the "back room" near the door which led outside to the backyard.

The house had a large back yard and a good portion of it was given over to a vegetable garden. Dad had helped his grandfather in the garden as a boy and had learned something about growing things then, but mostly, he was a self-taught gardener. He turned the soil with a hand cultivator and planted all kinds of vegetables. There were tomatoes, peas, beans, cucumbers, carrots, radishes, potatoes, squash, and several rows of sweet corn. We ate vegetables from the garden all summer and during corn season, we ate that almost every night.

I can still hear my father's voice telling my mother to "put the corn water on" as he headed out the back door to pick it.

A small patch of the garden was allocated to Judy and me so we could have our own gardens. We enjoyed planting and tending these and then watching as tiny plants became full-grown vegetables. My success as a gardener was somewhat uneven as I sometimes would let days go by without caring for the plot, allowing the plants to become choked with weeds. Sometimes I was able to rescue them but at other times the encroachment had gone so far as to appear hopeless and I gave up.

Every fall, we would pull all the corn stalks from the garden and make a big pile along with the leaves we raked. We would put these on the strip of grass between the sidewalk and street and make a big bonfire. Open burning was allowed at that time, even in town. We would put potatoes in with the leaves before my father lit the fire so they would bake while it burned. Then we would roast marshmallows. After the fire died down, we would use sticks to pull out the potatoes, butter them, and enjoy their smokey taste.

My mother did a lot of canning, putting up jars of tomatoes, pickles, and jams made from our raspberry and currant bushes. She had to work hard. It wasn't easy taking care of an old house. My father worked long hours as a door-to-door vacuum cleaner salesman and she had to learn to take care of the coal furnace during the time he was away. She was a small woman so this couldn't have been easy, but she managed to do it. Laundry was done in an old wringer washer with metal tubs for rinsing and then hung outside to dry in summer and winter. Everything was ironed in those days. Judy and I sometimes helped out on washdays, more because we thought it was fun, rather than being made to do it. My mother was never a strict taskmaster with us. We did the usual kid chores like washing and drying the dishes and setting the table, and we had to take care of our room but otherwise didn't help out much with housework. It's not that we wouldn't have been willing but more that we weren't asked to do it. Mom had had a rather difficult childhood and adolescence, having to work hard at times and I think she wanted our lives to be more carefree.

Carefree is the way I would describe the years we lived in Marshall. I have so many memories of that house. I remember the many hours I spent sitting on the porch swing with Judy or a friend. We would push with our feet to get it going and the clunking sound it made as it hit the side of the house and the porch rails could be heard throughout the house all summer. We had fun playing "dress ups" on the front porch, donning old dresses, shoes, and hats we kept in a box. On rainy days we played with our paper dolls on the living room floor, and on nice days, we jumped rope or played hopscotch on the sidewalk in front of the house. We loved speeding down our hill on our roller skates in the summer or sleds in the winter, making a sharp turn at the bottom to avoid going into the cross street.

Most evenings were spent watching television. In those early days of TV, there weren't many channels but the one or two we had seemed to have all the good programs. Household favorites were *The Jack Benny Program*, *Our Miss Brooks*, *I Love Lucy*, and *The Ed Sullivan Show*. We all watched together, Mom and Dad on the sofa and Judy and I on the floor, right in front of the set. Often my mother would put out a small bowl of candy – the prepackaged kind like nonpareils or bridge mix for us to snack on. Judy and I always dove into it and, despite Mom telling us to "leave some for someone else," ate it almost non-stop until it was gone. Once in a while, Dad would make popcorn for us, popping it in a frying pan on top of the gas stove. We would hear the corn being poured into the pan and then the banging and scraping noises as he shook the pan over the flame. Before long, the kernels would begin to pop and our mouths would water in anticipation as the air filled with a delicious aroma.

We usually didn't watch TV during the day, except for Saturday mornings, when we sat on the floor, sometimes with a friend or two, watching programs like *The Lone*

Ranger, Sky King, and The Sealtest *Big Top.* We spent most of the morning watching until Mom entered the living room and, switching off the set, sent us outside.

I loved to read and spent many hours sitting on the porch swing or living room sofa reading books I got from the library or from my small collection. I read all the Bobbsey Twins books, some more than once, and also loved the Honey Bunch series, stories about an adventurous young girl of that name.

Among my favorite memories is a surprise birthday party Judy and I threw for our mother. We came up with the idea one day, and, without giving it a lot of thought, went all over the neighborhood inviting everyone we knew. We asked our next-door neighbor if we could bake the cake at her house. She said "yes" and, on the day of the party we went over there and she helped us bake it. That evening, another neighbor distracted Mom by asking her to go with her to visit a lady who lived up the street. While they were gone, Judy and I put the leaves on our dining room table and found a tablecloth to fit it. We hadn't really kept track of the number of people we invited and our small cake would never have served them all. Fortunately, my father came home with a cake from the bakery to supplement it. When Mom came home, everyone was there, and we all shouted out "Surprise!" as she entered the house.

I can still see Mom standing in the doorway looking at everyone and saying "Well, I'll be darned," which was a favorite expression of hers. She said, "I never suspected a thing."

Whether or not that's true, I'm not sure, as Judy and I may very well have let something slip, but, if so, she did a good job of pretending. I don't remember many other details of that party. Judy and I made Kool-aid to go with the cake and I think most people ate their cake and then went home, but I do remember how pleased my mother was. In the coming years, we would all talk about that party many times.

CHAPTER 4

THE AUCTION

W hen we moved into 710 South Marshall Avenue, the house was filled with furniture that had belonged to my grandparents, and something had to be done with it to make room for our own furniture, which was on its way from Buffalo in a moving van. Among the furnishings were many beautiful pieces, several of which had been passed down to my Grandmother Nellie from her own family, the Smiths. Grampa Osborn told my mother she could have whatever she wanted and she did take some of the china and a few pieces of furniture. There was a large dining room in the house that held a table and several chairs, along with a large china cabinet and buffet, and my mother decided we could use those. For the most part, however, she didn't want to deprive Grampa of the money the sale of his belongings would bring him.

Grampa wanted to hold an auction, but Dad didn't think this would be a good idea. He said, "Things sell for a lot less than they are worth at an auction, and besides that, we will have to pay the auctioneer. Why don't we try to sell some of the nicer pieces by a private sale and then maybe we can auction off what is left."

Grampa didn't like that idea very much. Once he had gotten the idea of an auction into his head, he couldn't be persuaded otherwise, so an auction is the way they went.

There was great excitement in our neighborhood on the day of our auction. Judy and I awoke to a beautiful June morning, and we had barely gotten dressed and eaten our breakfast before the auctioneer arrived, along with a couple of helpers. The men began carrying items out the front door and placing them on the porch and front yard as the auctioneer directed them as to exact placement. By the end of the morning, all of Grampa's belongings – antique furniture, oriental carpets, dishes, and household items among them – were spread about the property.

The auction started in the afternoon. People came from all over, and neighbors and kids from up and down the street came to watch. Judy and I had never seen an auction before and were greatly fascinated by the whole thing. We watched as the auctioneer pointed to an object or held it up and then went into a lengthy description of it, extolling all its virtues in a typical auctioneer spiel. He would then ask for an opening bid, "What am I offered for this beautiful (chair, carpet, or whatever the item was)?"

After an opening bid was received, he would try to get the buyer to go higher, "I have five dollars, do I hear six?" This went on until at last, he would slam his gavel down on a block of wood and shout out "Sold to the lady in the blue dress," pointing to a woman in the crowd. If an item didn't sell, it would be put in a group with some other items, which would then be sold as a lot.

Judy and I watched the auction until we grew bored and then began running around the yard, in and out of the furnishings, making general nuisances of ourselves and causing our parents to speak to us several times. The auction continued on as, one by one, each item was bid on, sold, and then carried off until, by early evening, the front yard was empty.

I can still remember my father saying sadly that, after the auctioneer was paid, Grampa only made about $200 from the sale of all his beautiful things and "if only he had listened to me." It was, however, the way Grampa wanted to do it and if he had any regrets, he didn't voice them.

After the auction, we were left with a nearly empty house. We expected the moving van with our furniture to arrive any day, but it actually took much longer. After waiting day after day for it to arrive, Dad finally called the moving company. An investigation into the situation uncovered the fact that the van had been misdirected and sent to another state. It took almost a month for our furniture to arrive.

CHAPTER 5
THE DEEP CUT

Directly behind our house on South Marshall Avenue, there was an area that Grampa Osborn called "the deep cut." The backyard ended in a steep inclination which led down to a valley floor. I had always assumed this to be a natural ravine but recently learned it was a man-made excavation that was done to accommodate a railroad needed to carry materials in and out of nearby factories. The railroad had long ago been discontinued and the tracks removed – probably due to the iron being needed for the war effort, and the area allowed to grow wild. It was now a deep valley with steep sides and a central path.

The deep cut ran behind all the houses for the entire length of South Marshall Avenue Hill sometimes called Capitol Hill. It could be entered, by those who knew the way, from either of the streets that intersected with that part of South Marshall – Monroe Street on the south, near Freddie's Market, and Locust Street, near Rice Creek. We always entered it by climbing down the steep slope behind our house.

At the top of the part of the deep cut that was near our house, a neighbor had made a swing by tying one end of a thick rope to an old tire and the other end to the sturdy branch of a tall tree. Anyone who dared could sit on the tire and experience a thrill as they were pushed out over the chasm.

The deep cut was a place where only kids went. I don't remember our parents ever going there, except perhaps to stand at the top and call for us if they wanted us and thought we were there. The deep cut was a place where my sister and I spent many of our summer days, often heading there right after breakfast. One of us would say, "Let's go to the deep cut" and off we would go.

The area was filled with all manner of bushes and trees, including wild apple trees and berry bushes. We would spend hours there playing and exploring. With our active imaginations at work, there was no end to the adventures the deep cut provided. Some of the trees were good for climbing and we had given special names to them. There was a tree that had grown up through a large metal structure that we called "Merry-Go-Round Tree." The paths had names, too. There was "Weedy Mountain," so named for obvious reasons, and "Rocky Mountain," called this because its many rocks provided good footholds for climbing to the top of the steep slope. At the top of Rocky Mountain was "Rocky Tree," our favorite climbing tree. The lower branches were easily within our reach and we could use them to swing ourselves up so we could stand on them. From there, we could climb to the top of the tree.

Rocky Tree was at the end of a backyard belonging to a large Greek Revival house called the "Governor's Mansion," having been built at a time when Marshall had hoped to become the Michigan state capitol. The house was owned by Mrs. Bertha Brady, an elderly woman who had retired from the Brooks company. Mrs. Brady was totally deaf but could read lips well. Judy and I had met her outside one day and we became friends. We loved to visit her and she enjoyed having us come. She couldn't hear us knock so we always did as she had told us and walked in the front door and wandered through the house until we found her. She was always delighted to see us. Our dog, Skeeter, sometimes went with us and she welcomed him into the house as well. She never quite got his name right. Due to a glitch in her lip reading, she thought his name was "Stinker" (he did have a rather strong odor, so that may have contributed) and always called him that. We tried to correct her but no matter how many times we slowly repeated "Skeeter," she continued to call him "Stinker" for all the time we knew her.

Mrs. Brady often offered us a piece of candy from a box or a cookie. Her house was filled with all kinds of interesting items. One I especially remember hanging on her wall was a "hair art picture," a design made from human hair and framed behind glass. Mrs. Brady loved painting by number and always framed her finished pictures and hung them up in her house. I had never seen this technique before and was fascinated by it. We were always interested in seeing what she was working on at the time.

The house had an old upright piano that we liked to play. Neither Judy nor I knew how to play the piano, but we pretended we did. We would sit on the bench and pretend to play some great piece of music, knowing she couldn't hear. We would run our fingers over the keys, dramatically lifting and crisscrossing our hands, like we had seen done on TV. Mrs. Brady would just watch us and smile. I don't think we fooled her one bit but she never said anything.

Our mother knew Mrs. Brady and sometimes she and a neighbor would walk up in the evening to visit her. After we moved away, we exchanged Christmas cards with Mrs. Brady for a few years until one day receiving a letter from her lawyer informing us that she had died.

When I reached my teen years, I stopped playing in the deep cut but continued to use it as a place of refuge from the world. If I was in trouble at home or upset or angry about something that happened, it was a place to hide out or just cry and be by myself. To this day, the deep cut remains one of my favorite memories of living in Marshall.

CHAPTER 6
SCHOOL DAYS

When we started school at the end of that summer, Judy and I went our separate ways. Now in second grade, Judy headed to Capitol Hill School, a two-room schoolhouse that had been built in 1860 and was a couple of blocks from our house. My school, called Central School, was farther away and attended by older students.

During that first summer, I had made a new girlfriend, who, like me, was entering fifth grade that year. Irene was a tall girl with long brown hair that she always wore in two braids that reached the middle of her back. She lived at the end of South Marshall Ave, near the Kalamazoo River, with her widowed mother and three older sisters. Over the next couple of years, Irene and I were to become good friends and have a lot of fun together until, during seventh grade, her mother remarried and the family moved to Battle Creek

We walked to and from school together, often stopping

at the Rice Creek Bridge to do somersaults over the metal pipe guard rails meant to keep people from the steep slope that led to the creek. On days we didn't have school, we liked to play in the empty lots along the Kalamazoo River, near where she lived. Irene's house stood on a corner lot and had a big yard. If there were enough other kids around, we played hide and seek, red light/green light, or Red Rover. On rainy days, we played inside, either upstairs in our play-room or at Irene's house.

In winter, we sledded on a hill near Rice Creek and went ice skating at the athletic field. Flooded every year by the fire department, the field was equipped with lights, loud-speakers that played music, and a small shed where we put on and took off our skates. We usually skated at night when it was often very cold but I never minded as my mother al-ways made sure I was well bundled up. What fun we had, zipping around the rink to the music, skating forward and backward, and practicing our twirls and spins.

Irene stopped at my house on the first day of school and the two of us headed off together, walking under the gi-ant elm and maple trees, over our hill, and across the Rice Creek bridge until finally turning left onto Green Street. I carried my new cardboard pencil box which contained sup-plies such as pencils, an eraser, and a small ruler.

Central School had been built in 1900 as a high school but when I went there, it was being used for students in third through eighth grades. A bridge on the second floor, where the seventh and eighth graders went, connected the building to the newer high school. The school was a large stone building with wooden floors and wide stairways. The classrooms, which carried the scent of pencil shavings and chalk dust from years past, had tall windows which were opened from the top with long poles with metal hooks on the ends.

My classroom had rows of desks with chairs attached to them by metal frames. The desks had hinged lids which lifted up to allow access to a metal bin in which books and supplies were stored. There were inkwells in the tops of the desks but we were told we wouldn't need them. We would need to purchase our own bottles of ink which would be kept in our desks. We were given our textbooks and instructed to take them home and cover them. My mother and I would spend the next few evenings cutting up brown paper grocery bags to be used as covers.

"Get out your penmanship books, a piece of paper, your pens, and ink," our teacher, Mrs. Sherman, instructed a few days after the start of school.

The penmanship books were small soft-cover books with lined pages containing the letters A through Z, both capital and lowercase, written in cursive. The goal was to duplicate these letters exactly as they were shown in the book. We inserted our pen points into our wooden pens and then dipped them into the ink, after which we attempted to write. Although writing with pen and ink looked like it would be fun, we found it more difficult than we anticipated. The ink often came out of the pen in a blob or ran down the paper, causing the need to start over. After finally completing a section of writing, we used our ink blotters to absorb the excess. We got better at writing with the pens as time went by but it remained a messy process, our fingers and sometimes our clothes becoming stained with ink.

When we got to sixth grade, we were allowed to graduate to fountain pens which could be filled with ink, making them more efficient but were often just as messy. The filled pens were designed to be carried in a pocket or purse but often leaked. Finally, when we entered junior high, ballpoint pens were allowed and most of us were happy to leave pen and ink behind

Central School was several blocks from our house and we always walked, no matter what the weather. We had no choice, as my family, like most in those days, had only one car and my father used it for work. The only school buses were used by the rural and farm kids who lived too far away to walk. These kids ate lunch in the school cafeteria where they could buy a hot lunch for twenty-five cents or eat one brought from home. We ate there occasionally if the weather was especially bad but, having an hour for lunch, usually went home.

Our mother knew what time to expect us and would have our lunch prepared and waiting on the table. Lunch was sandwiches – peanut butter and jelly, bologna, or tuna fish, always on white bread. We sometimes had soup with the sandwiches or, our favorite, Franco-American Spaghetti. This came in cans and had a sweet, tomato-ey taste and a soft, slippery texture that slid easily down my throat and seemed to go so well with a peanut butter and jelly sandwich.

Lunch was the only meal when we were allowed to read at the table and we always read comic books. Judy and I had a collection of these that we kept in a box and read over and over before sometimes trading them with a friend. I would eat lunch while caught up in the adventures of Archie and Veronica, Blondie and her family, or Little Lulu. It didn't really matter that I may have already read that comic several times, the stories were still good. After we finished lunch we would head back to school for the afternoon.

Back and forth Judy and I walked, four times a day, in all kinds of weather, hearing the fallen leaves crunch under our feet in the fall, slogging through the spring mud puddles, and winter snow and slush. Rain and thunderstorms happen at all times of the year. We never gave the weather much thought. We pulled rubber boots over our shoes and bundled up in snowsuits or yellow slicker raincoats to protect us from the elements.

I loved to roller skate and would sometimes skate to school in the nice weather. I had metal skates that fit over my shoes and were tightened with a skate key that I wore on a string around my neck. Irene would skate to my house in the morning and we would skate to school together. Once there, we would stow our skates in our lockers, retrieving them at recess and then again at lunchtime to skate home for lunch and then back again. After school, we would skate all over town, going wherever our skates took us before finally skating home, sometimes just in time for supper.

"Our class will have a sandwich sale next week," announced Mrs. Sherman one day that fall.

"What's a sandwich sale?" I asked one of my new friends.

"We all bring in things like sandwiches and cookies for other kids to buy," she said.

I learned that these sales were held in order to raise money to buy school supplies for children in other countries who were still experiencing disruptions caused by World War II. Bombed-out factories and roads were continuing to cause severe shortages in some places and children didn't have the needed school supplies. Each classroom in grades three through six held a sale once a year.

We got busy making colorful signs announcing our sale and then placed them in the classrooms and hallways all over the school. On the day of the sale, we all brought in our treats which included, not only sandwiches, but cookies, cupcakes, popcorn balls, and Rice Krispies squares. My mother made half-moon cookies which I priced at five cents each and spread out on the top of my desk.

One by one, each class filed into the room and walked up and down the rows of desks, looking over the selection. After careful consideration, the kids made their purchases and returned to their classroom to devour the goodies. After all the classes had been to our sale, we would have a chance to purchase some of the treats. My mother had given me a little money to spend and I'd had my eye on some delicious-looking cupcakes, hoping there would be some left when our turn came. Luckily, there were and I was able to purchase one, along with a Rice Krispies square. Sandwich sales were great fun and I always looked forward to them.

In the spring, after all the classes had held their sales, we would be divided into groups and our teacher would give each group some of the money from the sale and a list of things to buy. We would then be sent downtown to shop for school supplies. We would go to Morris's 5, 10, 25, 50 to $1 store where we would purchase things like pens, pencils, erasers, and rulers. We would then take them back to our classroom and pack them in small boxes, after which they would be taken to the Care office in Battle Creek and sent off to the children in faraway countries.

High school football was very popular in most of the Midwest, and Marshall was no exception. The games were held on Friday nights and were very well attended, not only by the students and faculty but by members of the general community. There was a lot of school spirit surrounding the games and most Friday afternoons, there would be a big pep rally in the school auditorium. I often went to the games with my friends, walking to the athletic field, which was on the edge of town. I had little interest in football, not understanding much about the game, but I enjoyed going with the other kids. Once there, we would sit in the bleachers and, bundled up against the cold and sipping cups of hot chocolate sold at the concession stand, enthusiastically cheer on our team. The school band would always be there and filled the autumn air with the boom of the bass drum and the blare of brass horns. Cheerleaders wearing flared knee-length skirts and long sleeve crew neck sweaters in the school colors of red and black led us through cheers. They jumped and kicked, waving red and black pompoms while we all shouted out cheers of, "Give me an M, give me an A" and "Push em back, push em back, w-a-a-y back," and sang the Marshall Fight song.

A homecoming game was held once a year and was cause for great excitement. There were many rituals surrounding this game, including the nomination and election, by the whole school, of a homecoming queen and her court. The young women, wearing formal gowns and tiaras were driven onto the field in convertibles during halftime and introduced to the crowd with great ceremony.

On the night preceding the game, a large crowd gathered at the high school for a snake dance. Joining hands and forming a long snakelike line, we danced our way to the athletic field where a huge bonfire was lit and the rival team burned in effigy.

The year that I was in sixth grade, one of the high school classes sold yellow chrysanthemum corsages as a fundraiser. These were decorated with the letter "M" and were meant to be worn to the game. Not having any money to buy them, Irene and I came up with the idea of making our own corsages. We picked hydrangeas from somebody's garden and attached pipe cleaners that we had soaked in ink and formed into the letter "M". The results were rather messy, but we proudly wore them to the game.

Team sports for girls were nearly non-existent in that era. The high school had a Girls' Athletic Association that the older students could join but there were no organized sports for the younger girls. Our fifth and sixth-grade classrooms had informal teams, organized by a few girls who were especially athletic. These girls arranged games between the different class teams and occasionally, teams from the other two elementary schools in town. I was not especially athletic and had little interest in team sports but joined because my friends did. The games were played after school. We played half-court girls' basketball in the gym and, in the warm weather, softball on the school playground. On one particular day, I was in line, waiting to bat, and stepped up too close to the batter who was up. When she swung her bat back in preparation for hitting, it struck me hard across both eyes. I never lost consciousness and don't remember "seeing stars" as people sometimes talk about after being hit in the head, but do remember excruciating pain. I sat down on the ground momentarily and then got up and, accompanied by a friend, walked into the school to seek help. No adult was present on the field and, I believe, the game continued as if nothing had happened.

We found my teacher, Miss Long, still in our classroom and she took one look at me and said she would take me home. Miss Long was a young woman who had begun her first year of teaching the previous fall. She was pretty and fun and we all loved her. She drove me home in her car but, when we arrived at my house, my mother wasn't at home. The door was unlocked and Miss Long found some ice in the freezer and made an ice pack, then stayed with me until my mother returned a short time later.

My mother looked over my injuries and said, "Oh my, you are going to have two beautiful black eyes." While concerned, she wasn't unduly upset as, other than some swelling and bruising around my eyes, I appeared to be alright.

There was never any discussion about taking me to the emergency room or calling a doctor. No attempt was made to blame anyone for the accident. I think it was assumed it was my own fault for standing too close to the batter. I'm sure Miss Long never worried about liability, either her own or the school's. I think the two women considered the incident one of those unavoidable mishaps of childhood. I returned to school the next day with very black eyes which took forever to fade but otherwise, no ill effects from the incident. Many years later I would have a CT scan of my brain and be told that it showed no evidence of my ever having had a concussion.

CHAPTER 7
THE ORCHESTRA

"We've been caught," said Esta. "Mrs. Brenner noticed some of the potato chips were missing."

"She reported us to Mr. Grey and now we'll be punished," said Susan.

Esta was the older sister of my friend, Irene, and she and Susan were both eighth graders. I was in fifth grade and it was my first year in the senior orchestra.

Several instrumental groups had been formed to play in a solo and ensemble festival that was to take place that spring, and the two older girls and I had been arranged into a violin trio. The groups had all been assigned to different rooms in which to practice and our room was a small cafeteria that was used as a faculty lunchroom. We practiced during the period immediately preceding lunch and, while we were there, the "cafeteria lady," Mrs. Brenner, sometimes brought in items for the teachers to eat with their lunch – one time a vegetable tray and another a large bowl of potato chips – and placed them on the table. The three of us had helped ourselves to these, moving the food around so it looked like (we thought) none was missing.

As I stood looking up at the two tall girls, they told an elaborate story about the punishment we would receive from Mr. Grey, the school principal.

"He locks kids up in his office and doesn't let them call anyone," said Esta.

"Yeah, and he sometimes keeps them there for a whole weekend," said Susan, looking down at me through her glasses. "And they don't have any food. Sometimes he gives them some crackers and water, but that's all."

They talked on and on as I pictured myself all alone, locked up in an office with only a box of crackers to eat. As ridiculous as this sounds, I believed them and started to cry. The girls immediately admitted they had been playing a joke on me and told me that while Mrs. Brenner had noticed "some little mice have been eating my potato chips," there had been no talk of punishment. While greatly relieved, the incident had only served to make me wary of these older girls and to increase my discomfort at being the youngest member of the senior orchestra.

I started taking violin lessons in Buffalo when I was in the second grade. I didn't have my own violin and the one I rented from the school had, of course, been left behind when I moved.

We talked about this one night at supper and Grampa Osborn said, "I think Charlie's violin is still up in the attic. Why don't you go up and try to find it." He was talking about my great uncle, Charles Boughton who, we learned, had played the violin.

A few days later, my father went up to the attic and found the violin, which was dusty and didn't have any strings but other than a few scratches, looked intact. He also found a bow that didn't have much hair and an old wooden case that was broken and didn't look usable.

My father asked me, "Are you still interested in playing the violin?"

I said, "Yes, I want to take lessons again."

Later that summer, Dad and I took the violin to a music shop in Battle Creek. The proprietor looked over the instrument and deemed it playable. He had me hold it up under my chin and said, "It's a little big, but she'll grow into it."

We left the violin at the shop and when we returned a week or two later, it had new strings and all the other needed parts. The bow had been rehaired and, because I had no case, Dad picked out a used one at the store. Per the salesman's suggestion, he also bought me a shoulder rest that looked like a little velvet pillow.

My parents made some inquiries and learned that, in the Marshall schools, instrumental music instruction started in fifth grade, which I would be entering that fall. The school music director was consulted and he decided that, as I had already been playing for three years, I wouldn't fit in with the beginners. He would allow me to try out for the senior orchestra, made up of students in grades seven through twelve. I was given some music to play and it was decided that I could play well enough to join the second violin section of the orchestra.

In addition to the orchestra, the music director wanted

me to take private violin lessons, to which my parents agreed. I began walking across town on Saturday mornings to take lessons from a woman who drove in from Battle Creek and gave lessons in the home of one of the orchestra members. The cost of the lessons, along with the other expenses associated with the violin, must have been something of a struggle for my parents, who didn't have a lot of money, to afford. However, they never complained about it, other than to threaten that they would no longer pay for lessons when I went through periods of not wanting to practice. I was by no means greatly talented, having just average musical ability, but they were proud of me and attended all my concerts and recitals with enthusiasm.

When we had company, my father often said, "Sandy, why don't you play your violin for us."

A week or two after school started in the fall, I began taking my violin to school three times a week. I would leave my classroom about forty-five minutes before lunch and go upstairs to the band room where rehearsals were held. There, I was given the last chair in the second violin section. I didn't really know the other players – they were all older than me. I wasn't one of those appealing younger kids that teenagers sometimes find cute and make a fuss over. I was just an average ten-year-old who was on the verge of entering the stage that some people refer to as "that awkward age." No attempt was made to make things easier for me, the youngest member of the orchestra, and I was largely ignored. The music was more difficult than what I had been playing but I knew how to read and play all the notes and understood the rhythm patterns well enough so, with practice, I was soon able to play it.

Later that fall, I participated in a district music festival that was held at a nearby college. We were given the day off from school to attend it and traveled to the event by school bus. My father dropped me off at the school early that morning and, wearing the required black skirt and white blouse, I boarded the bus and took a seat among the other orchestra members. As with the orchestra rehearsals, I was largely ignored by the older students. It should be said that I don't think they intended to be mean or hurt my feelings. They simply were typical teenagers who shared the same interests and friends and I was not a part of their world. I sat on the bus quietly while everyone talked around me and, except for when we were playing, spent the day by myself. My parents had been excited for me and when I arrived home that afternoon I showed them the medal I had won and spoke positively about the day, but was secretly glad it was over.

Later that year, there was a state festival and then, in the spring, the solo and ensemble festival. Some of the orchestra members were very talented musicians and they were chosen to play solos. The rest of us were organized into ensembles, mine being the aforementioned violin trio. As part of the preparation for that festival, we were all to play our pieces for the other students at two school assemblies. One assembly for the elementary school kids and one for the high school students, these were dress rehearsals, of a sort, for the main event. We weren't required to wear the regulation black and white "uniform" and were told we could wear dresses or skirts of our own choosing. The two older girls decided they wanted to dress up and informed me that they were planning to wear nylon hose. I had never worn nylons, had never even thought about wearing them, but, wanting to please the other girls, decided I would wear them, too.

I went home that day and told my mother that I "had to" have nylons for the concert. She was rather perplexed and wasn't sure if we could find them to fit me. I was probably of average height for my age but very thin with skinny legs. She took me downtown to a dress shop where we were sold a pair of nylons in my size. How to hold them up presented another dilemma. At that time, ladies fastened the tops of their stockings to girdles or garter belts, neither of which would have been appropriate for a ten-year-old. My mother had some round garters but when I put them on, they fell down around my ankles. Always resourceful, Mom made a pair of garters from two pieces of elastic. When I put these on at the top of the stockings, I was able to roll them down to just above my knees where, we hoped, they would stay and hold the stockings up.

I wore the stockings to school on the day of the elementary school assembly. Being somewhat embarrassed about wearing them, I hadn't told any of my friends. I hoped nobody would notice them but one of the boys immediately saw them and blurted out, "Hey, she's wearing nylons," causing everyone in the room to look. I got through the day and the performance went well. When I returned home and removed the stockings, I noticed a run and a big hole in one of them. They had been expensive and my mother was angry that I hadn't taken better care of them. She refused to buy me another pair and when it came time for the high school assembly, I wore ankle socks with my good shoes. I was actually relieved. The stockings with their garters had been uncomfortable. They constantly slipped down and I'd spent a good part of the day hiking them back up. They didn't seem worth all the trouble.

The winter and spring concerts were more fun for me. The girls in the orchestra wore formals for these concerts and my mother had made me a long dress from some pretty pink fabric. I felt very important being up on the stage, under the lights, and thrilled to be surrounded by the glorious music of the full orchestra – strings, winds, and percussion. The concerts, which also featured the school band, were held in the evening, in the high school auditorium, and were well-attended by the general community. Some of my friends attended with their families and, of course, my parents and Judy were always there.

For the rest of that year and the one that followed, I remained the youngest orchestra member. When I reached seventh grade, things began to change. Little by little, kids my age, some of them my friends, started to join both the band and the orchestra and I began having more fun. We traveled to music festivals all over our part of the state and, one time, even visited the Conn Instrument Company in Elkhart, Indiana for a tour. The Marshall High School band and orchestra were considered to be among the best in the state at that time and we often placed first in competitions. I came to greatly enjoy the festivals as well as the concerts. I played in the senior orchestra for the whole time I lived in Marshall.

CHAPTER 8
CLEAR LAKE CAMP

Clear Lake Camp
Dowling, Michigan
January 13, 1953

Dear Mommy, Daddy, and Judy,

Please don't mind the writing in my last letter. I had to hurry and go to lunch and wanted to get the letter off. I am having a very good time at camp. We have to take showers every other night, one night the girls on the top bunks take one and the next night the ones on the bottom bunks take one. It is a beautiful camp and I like it very much. All the girls sleep in one bunk room and all the boys sleep in one bunk room.

I like the food very much. When we get into bed at night, our camp leader tells us a story. We are going on a cookout tomorrow. We made ice cream today and are going to square dance tonight. The camp has a bank and store in the basement. It is rest period and Misses Spooner just said

to lie down for the last 25 minutes so now I will say goodbye
to you.

Love,
Sandy

The above letter was found in a box of family mementos.
Written in pencil in my fifth-grade cursive penmanship,
it is the only letter of several I wrote from camps to have
survived the years. Owned by the Battle Creek schools,
Clear Lake Camp had been a gift from the W.K. Kellogg
Foundation as a way to promote health and outdoor education among school children. Fifth and Sixth graders in
the Marshall schools were given the opportunity to attend
a week of fall or winter camp for a small fee. I remember
excitedly bringing home the permission forms immediately
after I learned of the camp. My parents readily agreed to
sign them and pay the small fee so I could attend.

I had never attended any type of camp and didn't really know what to expect, but looked forward to it with
excitement. Finally, in January, the day arrived and we all
boarded a school bus and made the one-hour trip to Clear
Lake camp. The camp was on a lake and had all the features of any other camp, including arts and crafts, a camp
store, and rotating kitchen duty. Instead of the small cabins
or tents one would usually sleep in at summer camp, this
camp consisted of a large, all-inclusive building with a main
activity room, kitchen and dining room, shower rooms, and
bunk rooms for sleeping. Instead of packing bathing suits

and shorts, as one would for summer camp, we brought snowsuits, winter boots, and ice skates, as much of our time was spent outside in the snow.

The first night at the camp was difficult for me. I had never been away from home before and I remember lying in my top bunk bed in the dark with tears in my eyes. I missed my Mom and Dad terribly and wanted to be home. I decided that the next day I would fake an illness and ask to be taken home. Morning arrived and I soon forgot all about the plan as I became involved in the activities of the camp.

We were kept busy most of the time. The counselors were mostly students from a nearby college and they came up with fun activities for us to do. One of the counselors, Miss Nancy Long, would become my sixth-grade teacher the following year. She was the teacher who drove me home and cared for me after I was injured in the soft-ball accident. Arts and crafts involved things like painting and drawing, making items using materials found in nature, and weaving long strands of plastic cords into things like jewelry or key holders. We played circle games like A Tisket A Tasket in the large room and bundled up for time outdoors.

We were permitted to bring a small amount of money to the camp and were required to deposit any we brought into the camp bank. The campers all had to take a turn working in the bank or store, which were both located in the basement of the building. Every day after lunch, we were given time to go to the store. Once there, we could draw out some of our money from the bank and use it to purchase items from the store. Most of us bought candy bars, which had to be eaten right there in the store. I suppose they didn't want us stashing it away to be eaten at some inappropriate time like before a meal or at night after we had brushed our teeth. Nor did they want the grounds littered with the wrappers. We would sit or stand in the store, talking and laughing as we enjoyed our purchases.

A lot of our time was spent outside. We skated on the ice-covered lake, played in the snow, and hiked on snow-covered paths in the woods. On the day of our cookout, we went in groups to the kitchen and prepared our meals. We put a hamburger patty, along with sliced carrots and potatoes on a piece of aluminum foil and then folded them over. These "foil dinners" were then carried into the woods where they were cooked over an open fire before we sat in the snow and ate them.

After the evening meal, we always stayed at our tables for a sing-along. We sang old favorites we already knew like "I've Been Working on the Railroad" and "You Are My Sunshine," as well as new ones that we learned. A favorite was "Kookaburra," an Australian children's song that was sung as a round. Besides singing, we were told stories by the camp counselors. Paul Bunyan was a popular folk hero in the Midwest and we all loved hearing the stories about the giant woodsman and his mighty blue ox, Babe.

The week passed quickly and before we knew it, we were back in school. We hadn't missed much schoolwork as two teachers had accompanied us to camp and given daily lessons. These, as well as the nature activities led by the camp counselors, allowed us to keep up with our school curriculum. The kids who stayed behind had had a good week too, as the teachers had planned fun activities to make up for them not going to camp.

I went to the camp in sixth grade, too, at that time, in late October when we did a lot of fall activities like leaf collecting and scavenger hunts. One night, we all piled onto a wagon for a hay ride through the woods, stopping along the way for a campfire, where a counselor told us ghost stories. Judy also attended Clear Lake Camp in fifth grade but had to miss it the following year due to a bad case of measles. She has the same fond memories of the camp that I do. In the years that followed, I would attend other camps, always in the summer, and while I would enjoy them, nothing would ever compare to the fun I had at Clear Lake Camp.

Parents Harold and Arnette Baldwin Syracuse, NY 1940

Baldwin sisters Buffalo, NY 1950

Judy 1953

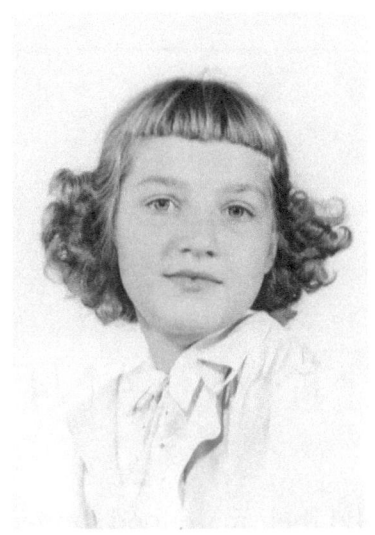

Sandra 1953

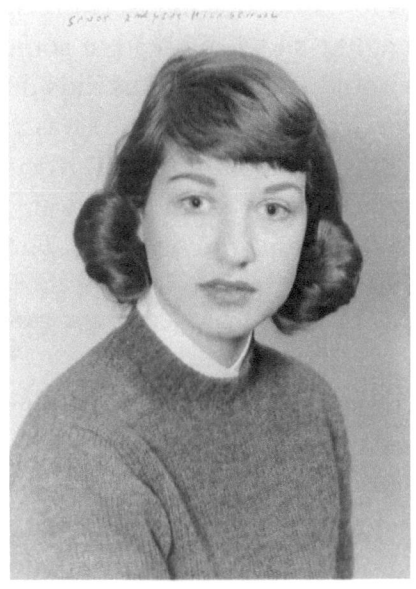

Sandra 1957

CHAPTER 9
PENNY CANDY

My parents did their main food shopping at one of the larger grocery stores in town. My father would drive my mother there once a week and she would get everything that was needed for the following week. If she needed anything in between, like a loaf of bread or something else she ran out of, she would send one of us kids down the hill to Freddie's Self-Service Market. Freddie's was a smaller neighborhood store that had all the usual groceries, although they were more expensive than they were at the larger stores, and there wasn't as much variety. They also sold ice cream, individual bottles of soda pop, and a large selection of candy. Freddie's was where we went if we had a little money to spend.

My sister Judy and I each received an allowance of thirty-five cents a week. We had to put at least ten cents in our banks but were free to spend the rest as we chose. Most of it was spent at Freddie's on penny candy. The store had only one counter and next to it was a shelf containing the penny candy. There was a large assortment of things like bubble gum, licorice whips, root beer barrels, malted milk balls, and strips of paper containing candy pills. There were also several wax items such as lips, teeth, and mustaches that could be "worn" and then chewed like gum, as well as small wax bottles filled with sweet liquid.

The candy counter was self-service and we would paw through the items, most of them unwrapped, picking something up and putting it back until we had made our selections. If another customer was waiting to be cashed out, the clerk would tell us to hurry up but otherwise would simply stand and watch us until we made a decision. We usually spent a few cents at a time, returning each day (or sometimes later the same day) until the money was gone. The allowance usually lasted no more than three or four days, and then we would be thinking of a way to get more. Occasionally we would earn a nickel or dime by doing some extra chore or would find a couple of pennies someone had dropped. This found money usually went to candy.

One day, when I was about eleven, we found several soda bottles that had been left by some workmen who had been repairing the railroad tracks. We turned them in for the two cents deposit and, of course, used the money for candy. This gave us the idea to try to find more bottles and we scoured the neighborhood, looking for some that might have been left. When we couldn't find any, we started going door-to-door, asking neighbors for them, but didn't have any luck. People didn't buy a lot of soda in those days and, if they did, wanted to return the empty bottles themselves and get the deposits.

A day or so later, Judy and I, along with a young neighbor boy, were walking past Freddie's and saw a soda truck parked outside. The truck had open sides and inside we could see cartons of empty bottles. We then had a brilliant idea. We could take a few of the bottles, wait for the truck to leave, and then turn the bottles in for the deposit. We figured the driver wouldn't miss them. We each reached in and snatched a few of the bottles and then ran off down the street. We sat on the grass nearby, watching the truck and waiting for it to leave for what seemed like hours but was probably only several minutes. When it seemed the driver was never going to leave the store, we grew impatient and, tired of waiting, took the bottles into the store, cashed them in, and bought candy with the money. The clerk looked at the bottles and then at us, probably thinking she didn't remember us ever buying that kind of soda (Vernor's Ginger Ale) but didn't say anything. The truck driver was talking to the store owner at the time and he turned and looked at us but nothing was said. We left the store, feeling our caper had been a great success. It wasn't yet time for lunch and the three of us went our separate ways.

I was the first to arrive home and my mother was at the door waiting for me. Apparently, the truck driver had known the bottles were his and reported it to the clerk who then called my mother. I made up a story about another kid giving us the bottles and she seemed to believe me at first. Judy and the neighbor boy arrived a short time later and she asked them about the bottles. Before I could say anything, they blurted out a confession. My mother was then very angry, not only about the theft but the fact that I had lied. I was the oldest and it was assumed the whole thing had been my idea (it had been). I was considered the ring leader who had led the younger kids into a life of crime.

The neighbor boy was sent home and his mother called. Judy and I were sent to our room to await our father's return from work. When he arrived, he came upstairs and asked us about it but didn't say much. My mother was the family disciplinarian.

As punishment, we had to spend the evening in our room and would not be allowed to watch TV. We would also forfeit our allowance until we had paid back the stolen money. Judy and I spent some of the evening discussing what we had done and our current dilemma. We didn't see how we could ever go into Freddie's again. It would be too embarrassing. We made a solemn vow that night never to darken the door of the store again, but, of course, we didn't keep the vow. We soon forgot all about it and when our allowance was reinstated in a week or two, we were back at Freddie's buying penny candy.

CHAPTER 10
HOME PERMANENTS

Judy and I both started out life as little girls with curly
blonde hair. As we grew older, our hair darkened and
straightened, ending up a wavy brown. While there is no
reason that this should not have been perfectly acceptable,
our mother seemed to think all little girls should have curly
hair.

The way to achieve curls in those days was to "set" the
hair on curlers. After washing our hair in the kitchen sink,
we would sit while our mother patiently combed out sections of hair and rolled them up on curlers. The whole
thing would then be wrapped in a bandana and slept on
overnight. The next morning, we would comb out the hair
into glorious curls.

The problem was that the effect was only temporary.
After a night or two of sleeping on them, or if we were
caught in the rain, the curls would straighten out and our
hair would revert to its natural state. If we wanted to keep
the curly hair, the process would need to be repeated on
a nightly basis. Because this was too laborious and time

consuming to repeat night after night, and our mother was unwilling to put up with our complaining that often, it was only done about once a week. Usually on Saturday night in order to look nice for church the next day or, occasionally, for some special occasion like school pictures or a recital. The rest of the time, we wore our hair clipped back in barrettes or fastened into a ponytail.

The home permanent was widely advertised as the solution to achieving beautiful, lasting curls and, periodically, my mother would decide it was a good idea to give us one. We would enter our house one day and, with a sense of foreboding, see the Lilt Home Permanent box sitting on the dining room buffet. We would try to forget about it but knew it was only a matter of time before we would be subjected to the unpleasant ritual of the permanent.

We would get up one summer morning, ready for a day of playing in the deep cut or running around the neighborhood with our friends, and come downstairs to see the implements of our torture set out on the kitchen table. Mom would say, "Eat your breakfast girls. I'm going to give you both a permanent today."

Judy and I would look at each other and groan. We knew there was no changing things. We weren't going to have the day we had planned. For the next several hours we would be prisoners in our kitchen. We would sit on a kitchen chair as Mom draped a towel over our shoulders and fastened it with a pin. She would then wrap small sections of hair with tissue paper and then roll them onto plastic rods. After all the hair was rolled, a cotton ball was dipped into a vile-smelling solution, which she used to soak each curler. The solution had a strong ammonia smell and the fumes made my eyes water, while the solution itself stung my scalp. I sat through this with my eyes squinted tightly shut and my nostrils pinched closed with my fingers.

"It smells horrible," I would say. "My eyes are burning."

"Oh, stop your whining," Mom would say. "It's not that bad."

"Yes, it is." I would argue.

During the time my mother was working on my hair, Judy would sit nearby, reading a comic book and not saying much. She knew she was next.

Periodically, there would be a knock on the door and I would hear the voice of a friend asking, "Can Sandy (or Judy) come out?"

Then, I would hear my mother say, "No, she's getting a permanent."

After all the rods were soaked, my head would be wrapped in a plastic bandana. My mother would note the time and then go to work on Judy. The time period was probably no more than thirty minutes but seemed like several hours. Every few minutes I would ask, "How much longer?" or "Is the time almost up?"

My mother always said "almost" or "just a few more minutes."

Finally, the plastic bandana would be transferred to Judy's now rolled head and Mom would return to me and apply a neutralizing solution, after which the curlers would be removed and my hair rinsed. It would still need to be "set" in bobby pins or curlers, but the resulting curls would then be "permanent," lasting between settings.

The next day, I would remove the curlers to find my hair was a mass of tight frizzy curls that was difficult to get a comb through. Because I had thick hair, the curls stood out inches from my head. My mother would reassure me that it would "loosen up" after it was washed. It actually took several washings and the smell seemed to linger as well. Every time our hair got wet, a slight ammonia odor would be detected, sometimes causing someone to ask "What's that smell?" or "Did someone just get a permanent?"

Judy and I, envious of friends who either had naturally curly hair or mothers who didn't seem to mind having daughters who didn't, could only breathe a sigh of relief once the ordeal of the permanent was over and hoped it would be a long time before we had to go through it again. After a while, Mom gave up on giving us permanents. The results were less than satisfactory and I think she felt it wasn't worth all the work and grew tired of putting up with our complaints. As we got older, we learned to set our own hair with bobby pins or clips and were allowed to style and wear it as we chose. The era of home permanents had come to an end.

CHAPTER 11
FREE RANGE KIDS

"It won't open. I think it's locked," my friend, Irene, said as she turned the knob and pushed on the front door of the library.

"Let me try," I said, moving past her and pushing on the door. "You're right," I said. "It won't open. It's locked."

We looked at the heavy wooden door. There was a keyhole but no inside latch. The only way to open it was by using a key. We turned and ran up the short flight of stairs to the main library room. Looking through the glass doors, we saw that the room was dark and, trying the knob, found it also locked.

"The librarian must have left," I said. "What are we gonna do? We're locked in."

We had gone to the library late in the afternoon, being unable to think of anything else to do. We'd spent a half hour or so looking over the books until the librarian had said, "Decide what you want, girls. The library will be closing soon."

We had each chosen two or three books, checked them

out, and headed down the stairs to the entrance. On the way out, Irene had said, "I have to go to the bathroom," and so, instead of leaving, we walked down another flight of stairs to the basement lavatory, where we spent several minutes talking and fooling around. During that time, unaware we were still in the building, the librarian had closed the library and left for the day.

"What are we going to do?" I said again.

"I don't know," said Irene. "Let's go back downstairs and see if we can find a phone."

We returned to the basement and, passing the lavatory, entered a large room filled with tables and chairs. We thought this room would surely have a telephone, but were disappointed to find that it didn't. We walked back upstairs and tried the door again. Still locked. What in the world would we do? The library wouldn't open again until the next morning. Would we have to stay there all night? No one knew we were there. We hadn't told anyone where we were going. When we didn't show up for supper, our parents would be angry at first and then worried. I imagined my mother on the telephone, calling my friends and asking them if they knew where I was, and then finally calling the police. I pictured a police car patrolling the Marshall streets, looking for me to no avail.

We were in big trouble. Irene looked close to tears and I felt like crying as well. I thought about spending the whole night in the library. Neither of us had eaten since lunch and there wouldn't be any place to lie down. We would have to sleep on the bare floor.

Getting out ended up being fairly easy. We pulled a chair into the lavatory and, by standing on it, were able to reach and then climb through the window, which was level with the ground outside. As we walked home, we talked about our adventure and laughed about it. It would be months before we would tell anyone.

Like most kids of that era, I was pretty much left on my own most of the time when I wasn't in school. My parents saw that my sister and I had proper meals, went to school, and did our homework. We had chores to do and rules to follow but, as far as our free time was concerned, we were on our own. My father worked long hours as a door-to-door vacuum cleaner salesman and my mother, besides doing the regular housework, made many of our clothes and canned vegetables from the garden. She had very little free time and, what she did have, she wanted to use to read, visit with a neighbor or engage in some other interesting activity. There was never any thought that she would play with us or plan activities for us to do. We were expected to entertain ourselves.

The 1950s were not a child-centered time. At the time it was said that "children are to be seen and not heard," and we were pretty much left to our own devices much of the time. We were expected to behave and we were taught the usual safety rules such as looking both ways to cross the street and not getting into a car with a stranger, but no one worried too much about us. Occasionally an accident would happen such as a child being hit by a car or getting hit in the head by a rock or some object like a baseball or hockey puck, but otherwise, one didn't hear of terrible things happening to children.

My mother rarely knew where we were on the days we weren't in school. We were expected to show up for meals and be home before dark but, otherwise, not much thought was given to what we were doing. We occasionally got into trouble, but because most of the people in our neighborhood knew us, our parents were sure to hear about it when we did.

Judy and I would head outside in the morning and look for any friends who might be around. Sometimes we stayed in our immediate neighborhood, organizing games or playing on the porch with our dolls. Other times we would spend part of the day playing in the deep cut or head for the nearby Capitol Hill school playground or the county fairgrounds. Often we traveled farther afield, wandering all over town. The library was a favorite place to go as was downtown. Michigan Avenue had a large variety of stores and, although we seldom had money to spend, we liked going into the stores and looking around. If we did have a little money, we could spend five cents for a cherry Coke at Peck's Drug Store soda fountain or four cents for a jelly donut at the bakery. If we had lost our skate key, we could get a new one for five cents at the hardware store.

Our favorite store was Morris's 5, 10, 25, 50 to $1 store. Morris's had a large variety of merchandise including inexpensive toys, clothes, jewelry, and cosmetics. We went there to do our Christmas shopping, buying socks and handkerchiefs for our father and Evening in Paris perfume for Mom. On occasion, we would earn some money from a lemonade stand or be gifted a dollar or two by a visiting relative. We often spent that money at Morris's which had a selection of cheap toys, like rubber balls, jump ropes, Jax, "bubble stuff," and pick-up sticks. We were fond of wooden paddles with small balls attached to them by elastic bands. The bands always broke on the first or second day, causing the toys to become useless. In spite of this, we continued to buy them with the same unfortunate result.

Morris's also sold comic books, which were displayed on racks on the front wall of the store. Under the racks was a row of chairs where we often sat for lengthy periods, reading the latest issue of Bugs Bunny, Archie, or Little Lulu. On occasion, we bought one for ten cents, but usually, we just read them there. The store clerks would glance at us but I don't remember anything being said to us.

The store sold small pets like parakeets, fish, and turtles, and once got in a bunch of chameleons which they sold for fifty cents each. Judy and I were in the store during a promotion for these and watched as a saleslady placed the little lizards on various backgrounds to demonstrate the way they could change color. She also tied a small ribbon around one and then pinned the ribbon to her shirt, showing how the animals could be "worn" as jewelry. The poor little things must have been scared to death but that didn't occur to us. We only knew that we wanted one. Running home, we got some money from our banks and permission from our mother to buy them. We returned to the store and each bought one, bringing them home in a small box. When our father came home from work, he constructed a cage from a small wooden box and some wire screening. We were delighted with our new pets and named them Herman and Marilyn. We had fun watching them hop around in their cage and sometimes taking them out to play with them.

The chameleons refused to eat the special chameleon food we had purchased but we found that they would eat flies. We made a project of seeking out and swatting flies both in and out of the house to keep them fed. Unfortunately, the end of summer and cooler weather brought about the end of fly season and the chameleons soon died and were buried in the small pet graveyard behind our house.

We traveled near and far looking for new things to do and sometimes discovered new places. One day, my friend Irene told us about some "caves" that she knew about. The caves turned out to be old foundations that were under an empty lot near the Kalamazoo River. We crawled through an opening and discovered a network of brick cellars underneath that hadn't been visible from above ground. The light was dim underground but we could see well enough to find our way as we wandered from room to room, occasionally hearing a brick fall. Irene told us that her mother had forbidden her to ever enter these cellars and we could easily have been hit by a falling brick or become trapped inside, with no one knowing we were there. We went back several times, sometimes spending long periods playing there but never told anybody.

We sometimes climbed down the bank to Rice Creek and waded there. Leaving the water one day, I looked down to see two wiggling blobs on my feet.

"Leeches," one of the other kids screamed. "You have leeches on your feet!"

I stared at my feet in horror, frozen into inaction. Finally, one of the other kids, braver than me, pulled them off. I don't believe we ever waded in that creek again.

There was a factory not far from our house called the Woodlin Metal Company. In the yard outside the factory, there was a large pile of discarded materials. We were playing in the area one day and noticed some rolls of gauze-backed, clay-like material. We picked up one of the rolls, took it home and, after removing the gauze backing, discovered the clay could be shaped into small figures which could then be painted.

After we had used all the clay, we decided to go back and look for more. We returned to the factory yard and were climbing over the pile which contained all manner of discarded materials, including glass and pieces of sharp metal, when a uniformed man approached us and asked, "What are you girls doing?"

"We are looking for these," I said, holding up one of the rolls of clay.

"Well, you will need to get permission from the office," he said, pointing to the door of a nearby building.

"Okay," I said and Judy and I headed to the office.

Once inside, we explained what we wanted to a woman

sitting at a desk and she filled out a small slip of paper, which gave us permission to be on the property. Returning to the trash pile, we helped ourselves to several of the rolls and took them home, where we spent the next few days shaping the clay in small animals and people. We eventually grew bored with the activity, but not before filling every empty space on tables and shelves throughout the house with our artwork.

"I know a real hobo," Judy said one day. "His name is Hammer Handle and he lives by the railroad tracks." She and a friend had come upon him one day while playing near the tracks. "He said we could visit him any time we want, but he wants us to bring food."

"I want to meet him, too," I said.

The next day, while our mother was busy in another part of the house, we looked in a cupboard and found some canned goods. We helped ourselves to a can of peaches and some peas and headed off down the street with them. We walked along the railroad tracks until we came to the spot where the hobo was camped.

We found a makeshift campsite with various scattered articles, including a tent-like structure and evidence of a recent campfire. Hammer Handle was a small, disheveled appearing man who was not much taller than me.

"Oh, thank you," he said after Judy introduced me and we gave him the cans of food. "I'll have these for my supper."

We spent the next hour or so with him while he entertained us with stories of traveling all around the country by hopping on freight trains. He told us he had once been a circus acrobat and showed us how he could stand on his head.

When we went back again, a few days later, he was gone and the campsite had been broken up. Whether he was arrested, driven off by the authorities, or just decided to move on, we never found out. We never saw or heard anything about him again.

Not long after we moved to Marshall, my parents bought me a used bicycle which I used to ride all over town. Judy also had a bike and once or twice during the summer, we would go on what we called a "bike hike." We would pack a lunch and, after stopping at Freddie's for a bottle of soda pop, head off for parts unknown. We lived near the edge of our small town, so it didn't take us long to get out into the country where we would find a pleasant place to eat our picnic lunch. One of our favorite places was the Oakridge Cemetery. We would turn into the cemetery and ride through the network of paved roads until we came to a pretty place with some interesting gravestones and set up our picnic there.

We would sit on the mown grass, sometimes using a flat headstone as a convenient table, and eat our lunch. After we finished, we would run all over the cemetery, climbing on and hiding behind the headstones. There was never anyone else there and we had the grounds to ourselves. It never occurred to us that we might be acting disrespectful and we never thought of the place as being spooky or scary. It was just a fun place to play. We would play there for a while before climbing back on our bikes and heading home.

Mr. Van Zant was our next-door neighbor and was referred to by us as a "grouch" or a "meany." He was an older man who didn't seem to like us, probably with good reason. We were noisy and often cut through his yard, although he told us many times not to do so. Our balls and toys also had a habit of making their way into his yard. He was always yelling at us or complaining to our parents about us. He had a grape arbor behind his house and, when we thought we could get away with it, we liked to sneak over and help ourselves to some of the delicious Concord grapes. He also had a small apple orchard in the back and we would sometimes climb the fence and pick an apple or two. We had climbed over the fence one day and were in the process of shaking one of the branches to bring down some apples when we heard him yell, "Hey, what are you doing?" Unknown to us, he had been working in another part of the orchard, hidden by some trees where we couldn't see him.

He came after us, but we were faster than him and quickly climbed the fence and ran off.

We ran and hid out at a nearby sand pit where we liked to play and were enjoying jumping into the pit when we saw our father's car pull up. He motioned us to get into the car and after we did, asked us if we had been in the apple orchard. We denied it, but he didn't take our word for it, and after driving home, walked us over to confront Mr. Van Zant. There was then no hope but to confess our wrongdoing and we were sent to our room as punishment. A few days later we got revenge on Mr. Van Zant by pelting the side of his barn with tomatoes from our garden. Once again we were banished to our room, but not before being made to clean up the mess on the barn. This behavior continued for the next few years until I reached my teens and my thoughts turned to other things, like boys.

CHAPTER 12
FAIR WEEK

The minute the announcer called for a volunteer to go up and help him on the stage, I eagerly raised my hand. *Oh please, please pick me,* I thought. *You have to pick me. It's the only way I can get into the show.*

It was the last day of the Calhoun County Fair and I stood in the bright sunshine on a small stage in front of the tent that housed the show of human oddities, in those days, called a Freak Show. Pictured on the front of the tent were the various people one would see if they paid for admission to the show – a fat lady, another woman with a long beard, a man putting a sword down his throat, and others.

The fair was held in the middle of August and for weeks before that, Judy and I saved any money we could in order to have plenty to spend on rides and treats. We also put great effort into earning "fair money." Our biggest earnings came from our raspberry sales. We had several red raspberry bushes in our garden and, after our mother had used what she needed to make jam, Judy and I were allowed to pick and sell the remainder. Most summer days would find us out back, picking the raspberries and putting them in quart baskets. We would then load them into our rusty old red wagon and go door-to-door selling them. As we sold them at a reasonable price, most people considered them a great bargain and they quickly sold out. By the end of raspberry season, we had over ten dollars in our jar. Added to our savings and other earnings, this brought our fair money to seven or eight dollars apiece, which we considered a fortune.

Judy and I always looked forward to the fair with great excitement. The fairgrounds were only a short distance from our house and every year, in the days leading up to the event, we would ride our bikes to the grounds and watch excitedly as preparations for it were made.

We'd watch as carnival rides and food stands were set up, buildings were opened and animals, handmade items, and garden-grown vegetables were brought in for exhibition and judging. There was a 4-H building where all the members of that organization displayed things they had made or grown in gardens. Judy and I were both 4-H members and we always entered items like aprons or skirts we had made and sometimes baked goods like a cake or cookies.

At last, it was opening day! The fairgrounds were within easy walking distance of our house and, during fair week, we went every day and spent the whole day there. We got in for free with our 4-H passes and would go in the morning as soon as it opened, return home for lunch, and then go back in the afternoon. We were allowed to go by ourselves and sometimes we would meet friends there, but often it was just Judy and me. Our dog, Skeeter, sometimes followed us to the fair and would wander through the buildings with us or stand and watch patiently while we were on the rides.

We went on all the rides, becoming dizzy from the spinning cars on the Tilt-a-Whirl and looking out over the fairgrounds from the top of the Ferris wheel. We went into the penny arcade and played carnival games like the Fish Pond, where we "won every time." We went through all the buildings, looking at the exhibits and checking to see who had won ribbons. Just being at the fair was exciting and we never grew bored. We walked up and down the midway, enveloped in the enticing aromas from the food stands as our ears took in the calliope music coming from the merry-go-round and the screams of the riders on the Octopus and Scrambler. We watched as cotton candy was spun onto paper cones and then walked away carrying the giant pink clouds, our faces, hands, and even our hair becoming sticky with the sugary treats.

Most everyone in the area went to the fair, so we always ran into people we knew. The fair was magical after dark, too when everything was lit up. As I got older, I was allowed to return there at night with my friends.

Sometimes my father rented a booth in the Merchants' Building to demonstrate and sell his vacuum cleaners. We liked to hang around the booth and watch his sales pitch. He would sometimes ask us to assist him with demonstrations ("so easy a child can do it") making us feel very important.

There was always something going on at the fair and we enjoyed watching events like animal judgings. There were a couple of sideshows and at intervals during the day, there would be promotions for these. The "girly show" featured heavily made-up women in flimsy costumes who stood on a stage, gyrating their hips suggestively, while an announcer extolled the talents and attributes of each. We watched as the women smiled and beckoned people to enter the tent and then watched a few people buy tickets and go in before moving on.

Of greater interest to us was the show of human oddities. The show featured various unusual people like the tallest man on earth, a bearded lady, a fire eater, and a snake charmer. There was always a "special exhibit" and one year that was a man who reportedly had a "baby brother" growing out of his torso. As with the "girly show," there were periodic promotions for this show, during which an announcer came out and talked at length about the show and what we would see if we paid to go to it. He talked a lot about the man with the baby brother, calling the pair "Siamese twins," and this was of great interest to Judy and me. We both tried to imagine but couldn't really picture what that person would look like.

Whenever we saw the man come out on the stage in front of the tent, we would stand and watch and listen to his entire pitch. We wanted to get in and see that show in the worst way but didn't want to spend the money, preferring to spend it on rides and treats like ice cream or candied apples. We watched the promotion many times and noted that the man always requested a volunteer helper to go up on the stage with him and that the helper was always let into the show for free. Each time he called for a volunteer, my hand would go up but he always chose someone else.

On the last day of the fair, I was ready for him. As soon as he called for a volunteer, my hand shot up and I began jumping up and down, waving my arm about wildly while thinking, *Oh pick me. Please, please pick me.*

As if he could read my thoughts, he pointed to me and said, "The girl in the green shirt."

I looked at Judy and grinned, then ran up onto the stage, where he began to ask me questions.

"What is your name, young lady?"

"Sandy."

"How old are you, Sandy?"

"Eleven."

"Do you go to school?"

"Yes, I'm going into sixth grade."

"Who did you come to the fair with?"

"I came with my sister and my dog." I pointed to Judy and Skeeter, eliciting laughter from the small crowd that was watching.

I spent several minutes answering his questions and listening to his pitch while Judy and Skeeter watched from below the stage. Exactly what was said, I don't remember. I was somewhat nervous and my mind was totally focused on getting into the show.

Finally, he said, "Well, Sandy has been a great help.

Everyone give her a big hand! Now you go ahead and go into the show."

I asked, "Can my sister and my dog go with me?"

Again, everyone laughed but he said, "Sure, go ahead."

Judy and I entered the tent with Skeeter trailing behind us. We looked at each other and grinned, not believing our good fortune. After the bright sunshine outside, the inside of the tent was gloomy and had a stale smell. We walked around viewing all the "human oddities." We saw the tallest man and the shortest man, the sword swallower, fire eater, and human pretzel. The fat lady and the bearded lady were the same person.

When we walked up to her, she smiled and said, "Hello girls, are you having fun at the fair?"

We smiled back and said, "Yes."

"She's nice," I said, as we walked away.

Then Judy said, "Where is the man with the baby growing out of his stomach?"

We looked around. We had seen everything, but the "stars" of the show were nowhere in sight.

"Maybe we should ask someone," I said.

Just then, the man from outside stood at one side of the tent and began talking about the "very special" exhibit which had been saved for the end. He again spoke about the twins but, this time said there would be an extra charge to see them. He pointed to another closed-off section of the tent. Judy and I just looked at each other. We didn't have any more money, having by that time spent it all. *Oh no,* I thought, dejectedly. *We aren't going to see them after all!*

By that point, however, we were determined to see them and, when several people bought tickets and then began filing into the other part of the tent, we just walked in with them. The ticket taker looked at us but didn't say anything and just let us go in. Maybe she was afraid of Skeeter, a mangy, black mongrel, who wasn't really friendly to anyone but us.

Whatever the reason, we soon found ourselves standing with a small group of people in front of a curtained stage. We waited there for several minutes and then held our breaths in anticipation as the curtain finally opened.

There he was! Standing on the stage was a bare-chested man with what appeared to be the neck and body of a small child, who was wearing a diaper, growing from his abdomen. The light was dim in the tent, compared to outside, but I could see well enough to determine that it did look like a real baby. We stared as he gave an informational talk and then invited the audience to ask questions. We couldn't think of anything to ask but several other people did.

After a while, the curtain closed and the show ended. We left the tent, our eyes squinting in the late afternoon sun. We figured it was probably close to supper time, so we headed for home. All the way there, we talked excitedly about what we had seen. When we got home, we ran into the house, the screen door slamming behind us. Our father had returned home to eat and both parents were in the kitchen. Judy and I began talking at once, about getting into the show for free and the man who really did have a baby growing out of his stomach. Mom just smiled and rolled her eyes.

Dad said, "That's fake! I'm glad you didn't pay for it."

Judy and I both swore that what we had seen had been real but after a while, I began to wonder. *Were they really*

Siamese twins or had the whole thing somehow been rigged? I never found out. The fair ended right after that and the following year, there was a different group of human oddities and the Siamese twins weren't among them.

The day after the fair ended, Judy and I always rode our bikes to the grounds. The rides would all be gone and the buildings empty, in the process of being cleaned before being closed up. We would wander through the buildings and scour the ground, looking for lost money or treasures that might have been left behind but, other than the occasional broken prize from a carnival game, we never found anything. Although the buildings would be closed, the grounds themselves remained open all year. There were people who lived in town who rented stalls in the animal barn where they kept horses. The fairgrounds were a favorite place for us to ride our bikes and we liked riding all around the streets. We often played in the grandstand, running up and down the bleachers and going up on the stage where we pretended to put on shows.

All that would be left for another day, though. After the excitement of the fair, the empty grounds were a sad and forlorn place that we were glad to leave, and we never stayed long. They were also a reminder that summer would soon be coming to an end and we would be headed back to school. Fair Week was over and wouldn't be back around for another year.

CHAPTER 13
FIRST KISS

"Do you want to dance?" said the tall boy standing in front of me.

"Yes," I said, looking up at him.

He took my right hand in his and placed his other hand lightly on my back as I put my left hand on his shoulder and we began moving around the dance floor to the music.

The community-building dances were held on Saturday nights and were attended by people of all ages. A small band provided music for a combination of ballroom and square dancing. When I was younger, I had gone to these dances with my parents and sister but, as I got older, I began going with friends. That night, I went with my three girlfriends, Sherry, Pat, and Gerry Lou.

Most of the time, we girls danced together but we were sometimes paired up with an adult for square dancing. If a girl was lucky, a boy might ask her to dance. My friend Sherry, a pretty blond who was popular at school, was often asked. I was a plain girl who boys didn't seem to notice and was seldom asked. Therefore, one can only imagine my complete surprise when this handsome boy with dark hair and brown eyes asked me to dance.

When that dance came to an end, we stood together talking. He told me his name was Gary and we learned we were both freshmen at Marshall High School although, not having any classes together, we hadn't met. We had gone to different schools before entering the area's only high school the previous fall. Gary lived on a farm outside of town and rode the bus to school. I lived right on South Marshall Avenue, not far from the community building.

We spent much of the evening together, talking and dancing nearly every dance. I didn't want the evening to ever end but, too soon, the lights went up, signaling that the dance was over.

Gary then surprised me by asking, "Do you want me to walk you home?"

"Well, I'm not going home," I said. "The four of us are going to Gerry Lou's. We're having a slumber party."

"Where does she live?" he wanted to know

"Not far from here," I said, explaining where she lived.

"Okay then," he said. "I can walk you there."

We retrieved our coats from the cloakroom and, leaving the building together, headed up the street with my three friends trailing behind us. It was a clear winter night with a dazzling array of stars. There was no snow on the ground but it was very cold, our breaths forming clouds in the frosty air. Gary held one of my gloved hands as we walked along, mostly in silence. The whispers of my friends drifted up to us, carried forward on the night air.

When we arrived at Gerry Lou's house, we stopped and Gary turned to me and asked, "Would you like a good night kiss?"

Taken completely by surprise, I was at a loss for words and said the only thing that popped into my head. "Alrighty," I answered.

I heard a burst of giggles from my friends and realized how stupid that sounded but if Gary thought so, he didn't let on. He smiled, put his arms around me, and kissed me gently on the lips. We said goodnight and, on cloud nine, I floated into the house.

Upstairs, in Gerry Lou's room, the four of us talked excitedly about the dance and, especially, "the kiss." There was quite a discussion about my answering "alrighty."

Sherry wanted to know, "Why in the world did you say that?" "Why didn't you just say yes?"

"I don't know," I said. "It just came out."

We stayed awake most of the night, playing records and talking. Every once in a while, one of the girls would say, "alrighty" causing us to dissolve in laughter.

Sunday was an endless day, the hours dragging by slowly. I looked forward to the next day's return to school with both anticipation and dread. I wanted to see Gary but, what if he ignored me? Did he really like me or was he playing me for a fool? I found it hard to fall asleep that night, even though I was tired, having stayed awake most of the previous night. In my mind, I relived the kiss over and over, imagining Gary's arms around me and remembering the way his lips felt on mine. I also continued to worry about what the next day would bring.

At last, it was morning and I was on my way to school. When I got there, I saw Gary standing at his locker, which turned out to be not far from mine. He smiled when he saw me and I smiled back.

When I saw Sherry in our first class, I said, "Gary just smiled at me."

She smiled knowingly and said, "He likes you."

I spent the rest of the day in a dreamlike state, not quite believing it was all true. *A boy likes me! I thought with some amazement.*

After that, we became boyfriend and girlfriend, although there were never any spoken words of commitment. It was just understood. Too young to really date, we mostly saw each other in school and sometimes sat together at assemblies where we would hold hands. We attended the same dances and parties and there were more walks home and more goodnight kisses. It seemed to me that my whole life had changed. I was now a girl who had a boyfriend.

I moved away the following fall. Gary and I had a sad parting and promised to write to each other. We did for a while but, with the passage of time, the letters grew infrequent. After a while, I found a new boyfriend and wrote Gary a heartfelt letter of goodbye. I never heard from him after that. I imagined him heartbroken but, more likely, he took it in stride and also found someone else. We would both move on, as kids always do, to whatever the future held for us but, for the rest of my life, I would remember the boy who gave me my first kiss.

CHAPTER 14
MORE MEMORIES

" This is the Marshall Airport and I'm calling to report the sighting of a single motor aircraft to the east and traveling north," I said over the telephone.

That call was made in 1957 when I was a member of the Ground Observer Corp, a cold war program organized for the purpose of "watching the skies." Citizens were encouraged to be on the lookout for enemy planes that might invade our airspace. People of all ages were recruited and trained to work shifts at observation stations around the country.

I was recruited into the GOC by my friend, Rosie, a lively redhead whom I had met when we had both entered Marshall High School as freshmen. The director of the local group was a friend of Rosie's father, and he had convinced her to join. Wanting someone to keep her company during her two-hour stints at the airport, Rosie had talked me into joining her.

Once a week, the two of us would walk or be driven to the Brooks Airfield, which was just outside of town. Once there, we would spend our two-hour shift watching the skies from a second-floor room with windows on all four sides. We took turns calling in and describing any planes we spotted to a central station, which in turn passed our information along to a larger center that monitored and kept track of those planes that were supposed to be in the sky and those that might be "invaders."

It was fun at first, but after a while it became boring. There weren't many planes and most of the time was spent just sitting around the office. We stuck with it long enough to earn our certificates and silver wings and then dropped out.

Rosie and I had met at the beginning of our Freshman year in high school and immediately became good friends. She was a middle child in a big Irish family and, like me, lived right in town, within walking distance from the school. We spent a lot of time at each other's houses and got to know each other's families. She sometimes walked home with me on school days and had lunch at my house, and I was sometimes invited to stay for supper at hers. I have fond memories of sitting around their big dining room table with all her brothers and sisters at suppers that were somewhat chaotic, but always fun, a change from those at my house, where the cranky and disapproving presence of Grampa Osborn tended to put a damper on frivolity.

Rosie and I had a lot of good times together, attending games and dances, drinking Cokes at Peck's or Hemmingson's soda fountains and just hanging around together, having heart-to-heart talks, mostly about the boys we liked, and speculating about whether they liked us. Rosie and I had our share of adventures, a couple of times taking a bus all the way to Battle Creek where we spent the day on the Goguac Lake beach, returning home, sunburned and tired in the late afternoon.

There were no public pools in Marshall but there were several small lakes in the area where we would sometimes go to swim. The closest one was Pine Lake, which was just a short drive from town. We learned about Pine Lake from friends when we first moved to Marshall and on hot summer Sundays, my sister Judy and I often pestered our parents to take us there, begging and pleading, "Oh please, please, it's so hot." Often they said no, wanting to spend the afternoon in some other way, but at times our persistence paid off and we were able to wear them down. When they agreed, we happily donned our bathing suits and jumped into the back seat of our car. We counted signs on the way, each counting those on her own side, to relieve the boredom of what was probably a ten or fifteen-minute ride.

Pine Lake was a small lake without a sand beach, just grass with worn areas of bare earth. It was always filled with kids on hot days. Our parents never swam but would sit on the shore watching Judy and me as we played around, practicing our floats, and jumping and splashing in the water. There was a raft in the middle of the lake to which one could swim but, in the early days of living in Marshall, we were forbidden to go there as the water around it was over our heads, and Judy and I were not yet strong swimmers.

The lake had a "drop off" and I remember stepping into it on one terrifying day when I was there with the family of my friend, Martha. Martha's older sister had been told to keep an eye on us but was busy flirting with some boys and didn't see us as we walked out too far and suddenly found ourselves in water that was way over our heads. I panicked, my heart beating wildly, and was flailing about helplessly when I felt a strong arm encircle my waist. Two older boys had come to our rescue, pulling us back into the shallower water. Gasping for breath after our near drowning, Martha and I looked around for her father, who was looking in another direction and talking to someone, seemingly unaware of the incident. After the sister's anxious pleas of "don't tell Dad," we made the decision to say nothing, nor did I tell my parents about it when I got home.

When Mom and Dad grew tired of being at the lake, they would wave us in. Never ready to leave, we would at first pretend not to see them and then beg for more time, but eventually be forced to leave the water. We would then wrap our towels around ourselves and ride home in our wet bathing suits. The lake had a small bathhouse but, for some reason, we never used it. I'm not sure why. The ride home was the same as the ride there except the change in direction put us on different sides of the road and we each had a different group of signs to count. One side had "Burma Shave" signs, a series of small signs which appeared along roadsides all over the country in the 1950s.

They consisted of a group of six small red signs that could be read by passersby. Each sign featured the line of a jingle. An example of these:

Your shaving brush
Has had its day
So why not shave
The modern way
Burma Shave

Judy and I always read the signs aloud in unison as if never having read them in the past.

Paper drives were popular fundraisers of the time. A scout troop or church youth group would get hold of a truck and driver and spend a Saturday going all over town collecting newspapers and magazines left on the curb by residents. We would ride in the back of the truck, jumping off to load in the papers and then jumping back on. By the time the truck was full, we would find ourselves sitting on the mounting piles of papers before they were taken to a collection station where they would be weighed, after which the group would be paid by the pound.

Judy and I once got the idea to have our own paper drive, thinking we could make a lot of money. We went door-to-door asking neighbors for their old newspapers and loading them into our wagon. When we had collected enough to fill the back seat and trunk of our car, our father drove us to the collection/weigh station where we were paid the disappointing amount of about fifteen or twenty cents each.

The paper drive was one of the many schemes Judy and I came up with to try to earn money at a time when we didn't have much of it. We were always dreaming up ways to make more for things we wanted to buy. We had the usual lemonade and Kool-Aid stands and once tried hawking leftover garden vegetables from the curbside in front of our house, without a lot of success. We made potholders on metal looms we got for Christmas and went door-to-door selling them. We once put on a puppet show, spending hours making puppets and scenery and then placing signs all over the neighborhood advertising it. We planned to sell tickets "at the gate" but the only people who came were a few neighborhood kids who didn't have any money, and we let in for free in order to have an audience.

Except for our raspberry sales, most of our ventures into entrepreneurship weren't very successful and it wasn't until I became old enough to babysit that I was able to earn a respectable amount of spending money. I started babysitting when I was thirteen or fourteen, minding the children of a couple of families in town for a few hours, usually on a weekend evening. The thirty-five to fifty cents an hour I earned would usually add up to a dollar or two. Much of this was spent at Morris's on things like lipstick, nail polish, and cheap perfume.

At the time I began babysitting, rock and roll was becoming popular and I, like most other kids, loved listening to and singing along with the songs that were played on the radio and on the popular TV show, *Your Hit Parade* which was aired on Saturday nights. The year I was fourteen, I asked for and received a 45 rpm record player for Christmas. Although I didn't have any records, I planned to use my babysitting money to start a collection.

When I had enough money to buy a record, I headed to the small music shop on Michigan Avenue. The store had a "soundproof" booth where one could play and listen to records before purchasing them. I selected two or three records, took them into the booth, and carefully listened to them, deciding which one I would buy. After playing each a few times and giving careful consideration, I decided on "The Green Door" by Jim Lowe, a popular song that told the story of a room that the singer wasn't permitted to enter and what he thought might be happening on the other side of a closed door.

I couldn't wait to try the record out on my new player and after parting with my ninety-eight cents, I walked home, carefully carrying the record in its protective paper sleeve. Once home, I put the record on the spindle of my player, watching in anticipation as it dropped down onto the turntable and the arm that held the needle moved over until finally coming to rest in the record's grooves. I waited breathlessly for the song to begin and then smiled as I heard the familiar drumstick taps and honkey tonk piano refrain of its opening bars. I knew all the words by heart and happily sang along with them. For a while, "The Green Door" was my only record and I played it over and over. In later years, my mother would tell me that hearing that song repeatedly nearly drove her crazy and she would cringe whenever she heard "The Green Door" once again begin to play. She confessed that she had secretly hoped the record would become scratched and, therefore, unplayable, but it never did. I eventually added more records to my collection but, "The Green Door" always remained a favorite.

No account of life in Marshall would be complete without mention of the visits to the famous Kellogg's and Post cereal plants. Both of these companies had their headquarters in nearby Battle Creek and offered guided tours of their facilities. The tours were popular field trips for various groups and clubs and a place people always took their out-of-town visitors. I visited them with groups like the Camp Fire Girls and when my grandparents visited from New York, we took them to both plants.

The Kellogg's tours started out in a room where a young woman, wearing a smart green uniform, told us the story about how the corn was grown in places like Iowa or Nebraska, with only best ears being shipped to Battle Creek where they were destined to become Kellogg's Corn Flakes. She then guided us on a tour through the factory, the atmosphere filled with the aroma of roasting cereal, where we watched the huge round roasters as they cooked and then emptied the flakes onto a conveyor. We saw cereal boxes being printed and then opened and lined up on another moving conveyor where they were filled with the corn flakes, then sealed up before being shipped all over the country.

At the end of the tour, which probably took about an hour, we went into a brightly lit room where we sat at round metal tables and were served ice cream sprinkled with sweetened cereal. As a parting gift, we were given a Kellogg's Variety Pack to take home. The Post tour was much the same, but that one featured Grape Nuts cereal and their beverage, Postum. It would be hard to find anyone who lived in Calhoun County during the eighty years the tours were offered who hadn't taken them.

CHAPTER 15
MOVING

"We're moving to New York?" I asked. "What do you mean?"

"We've always thought about moving back," said my father. "We never thought we would stay here forever."

"Now that Grampa Osborn is gone, there is nothing to keep us here," said my mother.

After my grandfather died, my parents talked about selling our house and buying another that didn't require as much work. We even looked at a few houses around Marshall, and Judy and I became quite excited about the idea of living in a nicer house where we would have our own rooms instead of sharing one. Suddenly, the plan changed and it seemed that my parents wanted to move away from Marshall and back to New York.

"But I don't want to move," I said.

"I like it here," said Judy.

"Well, we would like to be closer to the rest of the family," said Mom.

It seemed that, while they liked Marshall well enough,

they had never really been happy living so far from my Grandparents and aunts and uncles, who all lived in Upstate New York. Since Grampa Osborn had died, there was really no reason to remain in Michigan and they wanted to return to New York.

"Won't it be nice to live near Grandma and Grandpa?" asked Dad.

"You'll be able to see your cousins all the time," said my mother.

"Also, we think the schools are better there," said Dad.

Judy and I sat in stunned silence as my parents talked about the benefits of living in New York, but we didn't see things in quite the same way that they did. Judy and I, never having lived near extended family, didn't feel a loss at not seeing these people on a regular basis. Except for our Grandparents, we barely knew them. Every couple of years, our family made a trip back to New York and spent a week at my Grandparents' cottage on a river. My grandfather always took us out in his motor boat and we would fish off the dock. There would be gatherings with aunts, uncles, and cousins while we were there and we always had fun. Once during the week, we always drove out to the farm where my mother's sister lived and had fun running through fields and doing things like jumping into a pile of straw from a loft in the barn.

While we always enjoyed these trips and liked our cousins well enough, we were always glad to return to our home and friends in Marshall. In the years that we didn't make the trip, my Grandparents traveled to Michigan and spent a week with us there. I loved my Grandparents dearly and when these visits came to an end, I always cried, knowing it would be a long time before I saw them again. However, I always adjusted with time, busy with school and friends.

Judy and I tried not to think about moving away as our house was put on the market and eventually sold. We hoped our parents would change their minds but one day that fall, they informed us that they were going to New York where they planned to look for a house to buy. We begged and pleaded with them to change their minds to no avail. Off they went, leaving Judy and me to stay with friends. I stayed with Rosie, who was equally upset at the idea of my moving.

When Mom and Dad returned several days later, they told us that they had bought a house and we would be moving in November. Judy and I both cried and then began the ritual of telling our friends, who were also sad to hear the news. The kids at school were all interested in the move, saying that living in New York sounded exciting until I told them that, no, we weren't moving to Manhattan, but to a small town in Upstate New York.

I was especially upset about leaving Gary, my first boyfriend. Gary didn't say much when I told him I was going to move, but a short time later, he told me his mother wanted to invite me to supper at his house. His father picked me up and drove me out to their farm. Gary showed me around the farm which, unlike the dairy farm where my aunt and uncle lived in New York, didn't have animals, but large fields where crops were grown. Gary loved the farm, where he had lived all his life, helping his father in the fields. We took a walk through some adjacent woods where Gary told me he often hunted and he showed me a pond where he sometimes fished. I remember sitting in a rowboat on that pond, in the gathering dusk, while he told me of his love of the outdoors and we spoke about things we had never had a chance to say to each other before. We decided we loved each other and made a promise to write to each other and hoped someday we would again be together. After supper, Gary's father drove me home. That was the last time I saw Gary, except for brief encounters during my last few days at school.

Sherry was one of the best friends I had in Marshall. We had met in sixth grade and had been friends ever since. Sherry was pretty and popular. She was an expert baton twirler and when we reached high school, she became the head majorette for the school band. She had taken dance lessons for several years and a couple of times danced on the stage at school performances.

I don't know what Sherry's father did for a living but her family seemed to have a lot more money than mine. Their house was much nicer and Sherry always had nice clothes. She had three or four pairs of shoes, compared to my one pair of school shoes and she was one of the few girls who had "poodle skirts," flared felt skirts with large poodles appliquéd to the fabric. I was quite envious of that skirt and would have loved to have one but my parents, like many others at that time, didn't have the money for things like that. My clothes, while acceptable, were more practical and not replaced until I outgrew them.

Despite all her advantages, Sherry wasn't the least bit snooty or conceited. She was one of the nicest girls in school and always a good friend to me. I spent many hours at her house, playing records, dancing and talking, and sometimes spending the night. Unlike me, Sherry always had boys who were interested in her. She was with me at the dance the night Gary and I met and, after it became obvious that he liked me, she was very encouraging in our budding romance.

Sherry had her own horse, an auburn-colored gelding that the family boarded at a farm outside of town. Sometimes I went with her and helped her feed and care for Rusty and a few times she let me ride him.

On my last weekend in Marshall, Sherry, wanting to give me a proper send-off, invited some of our friends to a going away party at her house. There, the girls fussed over me, pinning a corsage of small red roses to my sweater. Sherry's mother had prepared a simple supper of sandwiches and salad and made a cake. After we ate, I opened the gift they had all chipped to buy – a gray crew neck sweater.

The party, which had started in the late afternoon, continued into the early evening and as the daylight faded, we turned on the lights in the room and Sherry put on some records. The music from these played in the background as the girls talked about songs they liked before the conversation turned to school, other friends, and upcoming events. I sat among them, listening quietly, knowing these things had nothing to do with me. I would no longer be part of that world.

Gerry Lou and Pat were at the party, along with some other friends from school. Rosie wasn't there, although Sherry said she had invited her. Rosie and Sherry didn't seem to like each other and, while both were my good friends, they weren't really friends with each other. I had seen Rosie a day or two earlier and she hadn't said anything about not attending the party but, while disappointed, I wasn't entirely surprised by her absence. At the end of the evening, I said goodbye to all the girls and that was the last I ever saw any of them.

A day or two later, on a gray November morning, I walked through the door of 710 South Marshall Avenue for the last time and climbed into our 1957 Chevy Station Wagon – my parents' first new car, purchased during a period when vacuum cleaners were selling well. I sat in the back seat, looking out the window through tears as we drove over our hill and across the Rice Creek bridge. We drove past all the familiar landmarks and as I saw other kids walking to school, I wished I could be one of them, headed for Marshall High School. We turned left on Michigan Avenue and drove through downtown and past the fountain, now turned off for the winter. Before long, we had driven past the city limits, leaving Marshall behind.

We settled into our house in upstate New York. I began attending my new school a day or two after we arrived and there was the usual awkwardness of being the new kid and adjusting to a different curriculum. The first few months were a struggle for our family. A few days after we arrived in New York, Dad was in a serious automobile accident and, as a result, was out of work for several weeks. As he worked exclusively on commission, he had no income during that time. My parents never discussed their finances with me but I suspect they had to borrow money from my grandparents to get by. We then endured an especially brutal Upstate New York winter. I was lonely and miserable, as was Judy, missing our friends back in Marshall. Even Mom longed to be back in Marshall but, as time went by, we all adjusted. I settled in at my new school and began to make friends and get involved in activities. My school didn't have an orchestra, so I joined the high school chorus.

My Marshall friends and I kept in touch through letters until, one by one, the correspondence with each dropped off. Sherry was the last one I heard from. She wrote to me a year or two after high school graduation, telling me of her marriage to a boy from our class. My family had talked about going back to Marshall during the summer vacation, but we didn't go. Perhaps it was due to the expense. Undoubtedly, the accident and resulting loss of income caused a financial setback. Or, possibly, my parents never intended to go, and this had been said in an attempt to mollify us at a time when we were very upset about moving.

In any case, we didn't go and I don't remember the possibility even being mentioned. Another plan I'd had, to move back to Marshall after graduation, never happened either. My mother exchanged Christmas cards with people in Marshall for several years and both my parents and Judy made brief visits there on the way to other places – Judy in the 1970s and Mom and Dad in the 1980s – but I never did.

I just kind of moved on and, as happens with most people, life got busy – work, school, marriage, children – the time flew by and before I knew it, many years had passed. I never forgot about Marshall. My memories remained clear and I would sometimes picture myself going back. I would imagine myself walking along the streets, maybe running into people I had known, but it never happened. Before I knew it, forty, fifty, and then almost sixty years had passed. As more time passed, I thought about how much the world had changed and realized that Marshall would have changed along with it. It wouldn't be the same town I had left so many years before. I began to worry that if I returned and found everything changed, I would lose all the memories I had of my years there.

At some point, I'm not sure when, I made the decision not to ever go. On occasion, my husband would suggest a trip there. He had been hearing about Marshall for so many years and wanted to see it for himself, but I always said, "No, it's been too long. Nothing will be the same." "I'll never go back there," I said the last time he asked me, but I was wrong. A couple of years later, I would discover something that would send me back to Marshall after sixty years.

CHAPTER 16
GOING BACK

M y father died in 2006 and among the items I removed from his apartment was a box labeled "Baldwin Family Photos and Memories." I had stashed the box away in a closet where it sat for over ten years until one rainy day while doing some spring cleaning, I ran across it and decided to go through it. Along with the expected family photos and memorabilia from my sister's and my school days, there was a bundle of papers pertaining to my mother's family. The small bundle contained several newspaper clippings and, most interesting to me, my grandfather, Philip Boughton's 1919 Army discharge document.

I had always known that my grandfather fought in World War I and that he and he and my grandmother both died very young from tuberculosis, but knew very little else about either of them. My mother rarely talked about her early years – I think it was too painful for her. I found a photograph of my grandparents that must have been taken in Syracuse, sometime in 1917, after they were married and before he shipped off to France. There they stood, looking directly into the camera, my grandfather handsome in his doughboy uniform, standing beside his lovely bride. Looking at that picture brought tears to my eyes. They both looked so young and innocent and I imagined them, full of hopes and dreams, not knowing what was to come.

I was filled with an overwhelming desire to learn more about these two people whom I had never known but who were an important part of my history. I began searching through newspaper archives and census records to learn as much as I could about their lives. I found my grandmother's grave in the Onondaga Valley Cemetery and the house in which she and her parents had lived when she met my grandfather. I visited the sites of the old TB sanitariums where Philip received care, and I learned about Camp Syracuse, the World War I recruit camp where my grandfather received his early training. I visited the museum commemorating the camp which was once located on the grounds of the New York State Fair. I obtained my grandparents' birth, death, and marriage certificates. I also wrote to the Military Records Personnel Center in St. Louis, Missouri, seeking to obtain Philip's record, only to learn that those records, along with the ones of many other WWI and II veterans, were destroyed in a 1973 fire.

Philip's discharge document lists the battles in which he fought and I began reading everything I could find about those battles and World War I in general. I made several visits to the Onondaga Historical Society's research room and learned a lot about life in the Syracuse area during and after the war. I started writing down everything I learned and putting together a picture of what their life must have been like. Eventually, I came up with the idea of writing a story about them. I knew the story would have to be part fact and part fiction, as there were some things that would never be known, but I wanted to tell their story as best I could. I didn't want them to be forgotten.

A missing piece of the story was my grandfather's early life in Marshall, Michigan, where he had been born, the same town in which I had spent five years of my own life. I learned that Philip had spent some of his early years on South Marshall Avenue, perhaps in the same house in which we lived, and that he was buried in Oakridge Cemetery where Judy and I used to eat our lunch during our "bike hikes." At that point, I knew the time had come for me to go back. I had to see all the old places and walk those streets again – the same streets that Philip walked.

My husband, Charlie, and I made the trip in July 2018, during the middle of a heat wave. We stayed at the historic National House Inn which is adjacent to Fountain Circle. Looking out the window of our room, we were able to see the fountain, which had been well-maintained and was just as beautiful as I remembered. The circle itself had a lot more traffic than I remembered and we found it somewhat perilous to cross its streets. On the other side of the circle, the house where I took violin lessons all those years ago is now a Chemical Bank.

The three days we spent in Marshall were brutally hot, but we did as much walking as we could tolerate. We walked the entire length of downtown and found the stores there greatly changed. Morris's 5&10 was gone, the space now occupied by a variety store. Peck's drug store was also gone, but Hemmingson's Rexall was still in operation, the original sign still out front. We went inside and found that they sold the usual drugstore items but the old soda fountain was gone. An employee told us it had been removed in the 1960s.

Most of the stores I remembered were gone, the spaces now occupied by boutiques and restaurants. The Garden Theater was no longer there, but the Bogar still stood, now a two-theater cineplex. Charlie and I spent a hot Sunday afternoon in one of them watching *Jurassic World*. The Brooks Rupture appliance building still stood across the street from it.

We drove around to various landmarks. My old elementary school, Central School, had been torn down and while the high school I attended still stood, it was now the Marshall Middle School. A new high school had been built at another location. We learned that the Marshall Redskins are now the Red Hawks. The old library, where Irene and I were locked in, looked the same. No longer being used as a library, the building was locked. I walked up the steps and looked through the glass doors. Everything both inside and out looked the same, but the ground-level window through which we made our escape had been removed, leaving a solid wall. The Brooks Memorial Methodist Church where I attended Sunday School and sang in the choir had become a performing arts theater, a new church having been built in another part of town.

We drove down South Marshall Avenue, stopping at Rice Creek, where a new park had been built, and continued up the hill to my old house, number 710. The house had undergone extensive renovation. The porch was now enclosed and it looked like a new room and fireplace had been added to the south side of the house. A modern two-car garage stood in place of the old one with its side-opening doors. As we stood on the sidewalk in front of the house, the owner came out and asked what we wanted. When I explained that I had lived in the house many years ago, he invited us to view the rear of the house, while explaining that he couldn't ask us in as his young child was napping. That was fine with me, as I had no desire to see what was sure to be an entirely changed interior, but was interested to see what changes had been made to the outside. When we arrived at the rear of the house, I saw that the old wooden steps where Judy and I sat and made friends with Skeeter were gone, replaced with a modern deck. A stockade fence now surrounded the backyard. The garden was gone.

The owner looked puzzled when I asked about the deep cut, finally saying, "Oh, there are some woods back there," while pointing in that direction. Of course, his child was now too young to play there, but I wondered if he ever would. Maybe the parents would think it was unsafe, or whoever now owned the property might worry about liability. We thanked him and then walked down the hill and looked at the other houses on the street. They looked a little shabbier but pretty much the way I remembered them. We looked down the next-door driveway and saw that Mr. Van Zant's barn still stood, badly in need of a coat of paint.

We crossed Clinton Street where Freddie's Market stood alone on the block. Long ago closed, it was now boarded up, the remnants of the old sign the only reminder of the store where we once bought penny candy. The railroad tracks remained, but the street was closed beyond them as a new Kalamazoo River bridge was under construction.

We went back up the hill, stopping at Mrs. Brady's house – the Governor's Mansion. The house was now a museum, owned by the DAR, but it wasn't open the day we were there. We walked through the backyard and looked down at the deep cut, which looked the same as I remembered. No children played there that day. We drove down the hill to Locust Street and saw that the entrance to the deep cut was now fenced off.

We took a drive to the Oakridge cemetery, just outside of town. I contacted the caretaker and obtained a map with the location of my family's graves. We easily found the Boughton plot and there they stood – the grave of my grandfather, Philip, adorned with a small flag, and those of his father, and brother Charles. Seeing the graves of these people whom I had never met in life, but were so much a part of me brought me close to tears. A short distance away was the Osborn plot where Claude and Nellie and their daughter Agnes were buried. The caretaker had placed a cone on an unmarked grave belonging to the family that I think was probably that of their baby son, Glen. As we drove out of the cemetery, I thought of the picnics Judy and I had there all those years ago, and my imagination was filled with images of two carefree young girls running and playing among the graves.

We had dinner our last night at the famous Schuler's Restaurant, which was still in its original location on Eagle Street. When the desk clerk at the inn made our reservation, she told us that the restaurant was more casual now, no longer requiring that men wear coats and ties as in the past. We enjoyed our dinner and then spent part of the evening sitting on one of the benches that surrounded the fountain, watching the changing colors as fireflies sparkled on the lawn.

I hadn't had any luck locating any of my former friends. I had gone to the public library that day. The new facility had taken over a building that had once been a grocery store and was modern and accessible. It had a nice local history section, which, like the library at the Inn, yielded a lot of good information. I spent a long time looking through the class of 1960 yearbook. I saw pictures of Sherry, Gerrylou, Gary, and many others I had known, who looked the same as I remembered them. I made a copy of the class list and took it to the Tourist Information office near Fountain Circle, but an employee there, a woman who had lived in Marshall for over thirty years didn't recognize any of the names. Of course, many of the women would have married and changed their names, and others had likely moved away or died.

The Marshall telephone book wasn't much help either. So many people these days have eliminated their landlines and aren't listed. I was finally able to locate a brother of my friend Rosie and learned that she now lived out of state but the brother was not in contact with her and didn't know her telephone number. He gave me the name and number of another sister and I tried calling her, but she didn't return my calls.

I Googled my old boyfriend, Gary, and found his obituary. I learned that Gary died peacefully in 2013 after "a long illness" at the age of seventy-one. The obituary reported that Gary had retired after working for thirty years at the Kellogg Company. He also continued to work the family farm, maintaining his lifelong love of the outdoors. Survivors included his sister, Sandra, two children, and two grandchildren. I was glad to learn that he had lived what sounded like a good life, but sad that the boy who gave me my first kiss was no longer in the world.

We left the next day. After we packed the car and I got into the driver's seat, preparing to drive, I suddenly felt an overwhelming sadness and began to cry.

Charlie then said, "I know why you're crying. This is bringing back the memories of the last time you left Marshall."

He was right. After three days of being flooded with memories, I was once again leaving the little town where I had spent some of the happiest years of my life. I drove out of Marshall, not knowing if I would ever return.

As it happened, I did go back a little over a year later, in the fall of 2019. I felt I had some unfinished business there. For one thing, I wanted to try and find Clear Lake Camp. I knew from doing an internet search that the camp was still in operation and was now called the Battle Creek Outdoor Education Center. It was raining the day we put the address into the GPS and headed for Battle Creek. The camp proved easy to find. After we parked our car, we walked to the main building, which looked exactly as I had remembered it. Lights were on in the building and as I got closer, I saw a woman standing inside. We knocked and she motioned us in.

I explained that I was a former camper and she was happy to see me. Amy Cherry has been the director for over 30 years and has seen the camp undergo changes, but many things remain the same. The camp continues to serve children from the local school districts, although there were no campers present the day we were there.

Amy gave us a tour of the main building. The main recreation room with the fireplace looked the same as I remembered, but the bunk rooms and showers were no longer there, a new bunkhouse having been built many years ago. She showed us the kitchen where I had done KP duty and where we made our foil dinners – they still make them! A display case in the lobby serves as the camp store where items like hats and T-shirts are sold – no candy. Amy took us down to the basement and showed us the space which had once been the store and the window through which we purchased our candy.

I asked about Wesley Woods, the Methodist Church camp where I had spent a couple of summer weeks, and she told me it was still in operation on the other side of the lake. She suggested we might go there that day and we did see signs as we left but, by then it was raining hard and we decided to skip it. Before we left, we took a walk outside and, in spite of the rain, walked down to look at the lake and surrounding woods, which I found as beautiful as I remembered.

We drove around Battle Creek and saw the Kellogg's and Post facilities, smaller now, as much of the manufacturing is done at other locations. I learned on the internet that factory tours are no longer given. After eighty years, the Kellogg's company ended their tours in 1986 and at some point, the Post Company also ended theirs. The reason given was worries about spies from competing companies stealing their secrets, but a woman in the Marshall Library told me she thought that the companies were more worried about liability.

I didn't have much luck finding Pine Lake. No one I asked knew anything about it. A Google Earth map showed a lake with that name just south of town but there didn't seem to be any roads leading to it. It seemed that the lake to which Judy and I used to beg our parents to take us and in which I almost drowned was now inaccessible and appears destined to remain only in my memories.

Our last day in Marshall was cool and sunny and we used the day to do some serious walking. Starting at Michigan Avenue, we walked the length of South Marshall Ave. We crossed the Rice Creek bridge and then headed up the hill. We found The Governor's Mansion once again closed to the public, apparently only being open one day a week. We crossed the street to the community building, whose cinder block facade was now covered with new green and white siding. A sign on the front door said that rooms in the building could be rented for events. We spoke to the caretaker and his wife who were working outside the building. They remembered the old Saturday night dances, the woman saying her parents used to run them.

We recrossed the street and continued down the other side of the hill, passing my old house. The street was empty of people – no children played outside. We crossed Clinton Street, passing the forlorn remains of Freddie's Market, the power plant, and finally crossing the newly rebuilt Kalamazoo River Bridge. My old friend Irene's house was still there. Now uninhabited, it appeared to be undergoing extensive renovation. I stared at it and at the river which flowed along beside it. I thought about Irene and wondered where she was, but realized that like all my other Marshall friends, I would probably never learn what had become of her.

We spent the rest of the day driving around town. Many things looked different. There were new buildings and some of the streets had been reconfigured. The old stone drinking fountains were gone. No one I had talked to seemed to even remember them. Charlie was driving, but I found it hard to direct him. Nothing looked the way I remembered. A new creek walk and river walk had been built and we walked those. We ate another dinner at Schuler's, this time in the more informal Bistro.

We left the next day. I did a lot of thinking during the long ride home, absorbing the changes that had taken place in Marshall over 60 years. Of course, the whole country had greatly changed during that time. I, like so many others of my generation, think of the 1963 assassination of President John F. Kennedy as kind of a turning point in our country's history. Looking back, it does seem as though nothing was the same after that happened. The Vietnam War was fought with all that it entailed, only to later be followed by endless wars in the middle east.

The baby boomer generation became a powerful force for change, both good and bad. Large corporate mergers led to factory closings and relocations. The drug culture, the AIDS epidemic, and the 9/11 attacks brought further change. The rock and roll songs that had seemed so ahead of their time when I was a teenager began to be referred to as "golden oldies," and were replaced with disco, heavy metal, and hip hop music. The whole world had changed during those years and Marshall had changed along with it.

I had learned during my visits that things had begun to change not long after we moved away. As was happening everywhere, buildings were being torn down and new ones built in their place, while others were repurposed for other uses. Small family businesses were replaced with big box stores and national chains. Friends moved away or died. The little town I remembered so fondly didn't really exist anymore and hadn't for a long time. As the rest of the country changed and evolved, so did Marshall, so that the place I once knew now belonged to the past.

Yet, even after all those years, the memories remain strong. I can picture it all so clearly. I need only to close my eyes and there I am, back in the little town where I spent those five happy years. I can see myself running through the deep cut with Judy, picking raspberries on a hot summer afternoon, and walking hand in hand with my first boyfriend under a starry winter sky.

ACKNOWLEDGEMENTS

I would like to thank the following people to whom I owe so much:

My husband Charlie Gowing for his love, support, and computer expertise

My daughter Kathy Warren who proofread my work

Granddaughters Isabella Gowing and Emma Warren who did the artwork

Teachers Linda Lowen and Carol Madar for teaching me the art of writing

Jess Neiding and Laura Thorne of Wildebeest for all they did to make this book happen

Marshall, Michigan, the place that gave me so many wonderful memories.

www.ingramcontent.com/pod-product-compliance
Lightning Source LLC
Chambersburg PA
CBHW030915140626
46545CB00017B/2365